Anglican foundations:

A Handbook to the Source Documents of the English Reformation

Tim Patrick

The Latimer Trust

ISBN 978-1-906327-53-8

Cover photo: detail of the manuscript of the *Forty-Five Articles* (1552).

Published by the Latimer Trust December 2018.

The Latimer Trust (formerly Latimer House, Oxford) is a conservative Evangelical research organisation within the Church of England, whose main aim is to promote the history and theology of Anglicanism as understood by those in the Reformed tradition. Interested readers are welcome to consult its website for further details of its many activities.

The Latimer Trust

London N14 4PS UK

Registered Charity: 1084337

Company Number: 4104465

Web: www.latimertrust.org

E-mail: administrator@latimertrust.org

Commendations

It is a mistake to live in the past, but also a mistake to neglect it or misread it. In the English Reformation we can find gospel clarity, theological and intellectual wisdom, spiritual richness, and a fine model of preserving the past while living in and serving the present and making the most of its opportunities. Tim Patrick's book will enable us to benefit from the English Reformation with more historical understanding and theological awareness. A unique and valuable resource.

Rev. Dr Peter Adam, OAM, former Principal, Ridley College; Executive Committee Member, The Gospel Coalition Australia

Tidy minds are in short supply, so we can be grateful for the work of Tim Patrick in this concise yet informative book. Here we read of the story of the English Reformation of the sixteenth century, learn insights about theology, politics, literature and publishing, and come to terms with complicated patterns of ministry, from which the modern worldwide communion of Anglicans has grown. This is not the moment to reject our ecclesiastical beginnings, but to seek to tell our story afresh, which Dr Patrick's clarity enables us to do. In the end, the Reformation is about worship, so the lessons of this book are immensely practical!

Rev. Canon Dr Rhys Bezzant, Dean of Missional Leadership, Ridley College; Director of the Jonathan Edwards Center Australia

The need for a comprehensive guide to the sources of Anglican doctrine has never been greater than it is at the present time. Unfortunately many of them are virtually unknown, their importance is not understood and they are often hard to locate. Dr Patrick has done us a great service in compiling a detailed index of them, explaining what they are, why they matter and where they can be found. This book is an essential resource for anyone with a serious interest in Anglicanism, both past and present.

Rev. Prof. Gerald Bray, Research Professor of Divinity, Beeson Divinity School; Distinguished Professor of Historical Theology, Knox Theological Seminary; Director of Research, Latimer Trust

For those of us in Anglican Churches geographically and linguistically isolated from all but the most basic of the primary and secondary sources of Anglicanism, this is a very handy resource which will alleviate some of that isolation.

Frances Cook, Lecturer, Centro de Estudios Pastorales, Anglican Diocese of Chile

Tim Patrick's *Anglican Foundations* provides a helpful exploration of the fundamental documents that define Reformation Anglicanism. At a time when many who claim to be Anglicans possess little appreciation of the means by which the English Reformers sought to convert England, this is an invaluable resource for understanding the variety of formularies used to pursue that end. Dr Patrick provides a sound guide for the reader with excellent bibliographical material for further research. This should be essential reading for any candidate for ordination.

The Most Rev. Dr Glenn Davies, Anglican Archbishop of Sydney

This is a splendid handbook on the various officially sanctioned formularies of the Anglican Church. Dr Patrick very helpfully outlines the primary sources, their contents and contexts, and gives us useful pointers for further study and reflection. An essential starting point for any investigation of historic Anglicanism and the Protestant faith established by the English Reformation.

Rev. Dr Lee Gatiss, Director, Church Society (www.churchsociety.org)

The first of its type in many years, *Anglican Foundations* is an excellent resource for someone who wants to know more of Anglicanism but is unsure where to start, for the interested layperson, and the seminary student contemplating a course of study toward their canonical exams. Dr Patrick gives a detailed description of the foundational sources for global Anglicanism as well as a bibliographical section for further reading that concludes every formulary. This book should be on the reading list of every Anglican in North America.

Rev. Canon Dr Henry Jansma, Rector of All Souls Anglican Church, Cherry Hill NJ; Canon Theologian for the Missionary Diocese of CANA East

At this time of cultural crisis, when there is so much pressure to compromise the doctrines of the Church, it is essential that we draw on the wisdom of the past. Indeed it is from this source that we understand ourselves and understand who we should be. Tim Patrick has assembled and made accessible the key Reformation documents of the Anglican world and has provided a learned commentary to help us place them in context and see their enduring worth. For this work all Anglicans will be grateful.

The Most Rev. Dr Peter Jensen, former Anglican Archbishop of Sydney; former General Secretary, GAFCON

For Gerald Bray,
to whom the church owes an incalculable debt for his work in making so many of the documents of the English Reformation readily available and accessible.

Contents

Author's Preface

The idea for this book came about during my doctoral studies when I was surprised to find that nothing like it already existed. As my research required me to trawl through the doctrinally determinative foundation texts of the independent Church of England, my first task was to identify exactly what those texts were. I knew that they extended beyond the *Book of Common Prayer* and *Thirty-Nine Articles* to things like the two *Books of Homilies* (which are, after all, referred to in the *Articles*), but I had little knowledge of the early English Bibles, and no idea whatsoever about works such as the catechisms and primers, or Erasmus' *Paraphrases*.

After spending considerable time coming to understand the formularies, I realised that an introductory handbook would have been of tremendous help in orienting me to the documents I needed to study. Subsequently, it struck me that such a volume could also be useful to anyone interested in understanding these texts around which the Anglican Church has been built: not only aspiring scholars of Anglicanism, but also those serving and living out their faith in an Anglican Communion which is currently both holding fast to its history and undergoing rapid change.

This small book is not a substitute for a reading of the primary texts, which it does not reproduce, nor does it replace the major secondary works. Rather, my hope is that it will serve as a useful guide for anyone who is eager to learn more about the documentary heritage of the Anglican Church.

I would not have been able to complete this work without the generous research provisions of the Bible College of South Australia and the invaluable administrative support of my Executive Assistant, Kim Folland, and Communications Officer, Brinda Ghose. I am most grateful to Gina Denholm for her outstanding editing and to the Latimer Trust for taking this volume through to publication. Thanks is also due to all who offered feedback on earlier versions of the manuscript, but especially to Professor Gerald Bray for his wise guidance, which has shaped the book into something significantly better than it otherwise would have been. This volume is dedicated to him. Finally, and most importantly, I am grateful to my wife Catriona for the unfailing support that she has given me in this work, as in all of my endeavours, and for the wonderful, committed partnership we share in life and in gospel ministry.

Introduction

In recent decades, the Reformation history of the Church of England—and, by extension, the Anglican Communion—has been studied in two different ways. On the one hand, traditional Protestant scholars have taken a top-down approach, poring over the official documents and writings of those inhabiting the upper echelons of the English Church and government in order to find out and understand what was promulgated for the realms.[1] On the other hand, revisionist historians have worked from the bottom up, exploring the realities of life in the towns, villages and parishes by consulting local record books, art and artefacts, and stories of local peoples where they have been preserved. The revisionist approach has challenged more traditional understandings of the progress of Protestantism by showing that much of what was mandated was never implemented or embraced by the people. Yet the newer approach in no way invalidates the older, but rather casts light on the period from a fresh angle and supplies different information. It remains as necessary to understand what the English Magisterial Reformers were trying to achieve as it does to understand the variable realities of religious expression on the ground.

The present volume contributes to the top-down approach by offering a sound and scholarly (if light) introduction to the full breadth of the Church of England's foundational documents, produced and refined in the sixteenth century when the Church of England was established and settled as a body independent of the Roman Catholic Church.

It might be asked whether such a volume is needed, as the formularies have been discussed by countless authors over hundreds of years. While this is true, there remains no single volume that introduces these founding formularies together. Subsequently, some of the formularies have received far more attention than others, with some even falling into obscurity despite their prominence during the English Reformation. So, while the *Book of Common Prayer* and *Thirty-Nine Articles* are very well known, the printed Bibles and homiliaries are less so, and volumes such

[1] Throughout this volume, when 'Church' is capitalised, it refers to the institutional church: the Church of England, the Roman Catholic, the Anglican Church, etc. When in lowercase, it refers to the church generally, the local church, or the church universal.

as the primers and catechisms are unheard of by many of today's Anglicans.

The problem is deeper still, as the formularies can only be fully understood when they are understood together as part of a carefully prepared matrix of documents, each one designed to advance the Protestant cause on a different front, but all in concert with each other. An illustration may serve to make the point. The individual formularies can be thought of as different cogs within the single machine of early modern English religious life. Each cog has its own integrity and purpose, but it is only when they are all working together that the whole machine becomes fully operational, and the particular contribution of each cog can be recognised. Taken out of the machine, each cog may still have some use and function, but it has lost its original setting and perhaps also its original purpose.

So it is with the formularies. That they were originally intended to work together is evidenced by the fact that Henry VIII, Edward VI, Mary I and Elizabeth I all authorised their own versions of most of these texts during their reigns. These monarchs knew that in order to establish the doctrine, discipline and devotion of the Church in a uniform manner, they needed to produce a full complement of formularies, each with its distinct role and function yet able to work in unison.

This guide provides an orientation to the different types, or families, of formularies and their distinct but complementary purposes, and to the individual examples of each type. Each of the first seven chapters in this book is dedicated to one family of formulary, providing some details of each member of that family. Chapter eight discusses two texts that were not written as formularies, but which were adopted into the suite of the Church's approved doctrinal works. Chapter nine provides brief notes on several types of legally important documents that could also confirm doctrine.

It is important to make the right distinctions between the different families of formularies. Failure to do so had led some scholars to make significant errors when commenting on the documents of England's Reformation. For example, Charles Hardwick in his otherwise excellent *A History of the Articles of Religion* mistakenly says that the *Ten Articles* were 'virtually superseded' by the *Institution of a Christian Man*, (*Bishops' Book*), and then finally 'supplanted' by *Necessary Doctrine and*

Erudition for any Christian Man, (*King's Book*).[2] While it is quite true to say that the *Bishops' Book* and *King's Book* postdate the *Ten Articles*, and that they moved England's theology beyond what was found in the earlier works, it is not correct to speak of the *Bishops' Book* or *King's Book* as replacements for the *Ten Articles*. To do so is to make a serious category error because the *Bishops' Book* and *King's Book* were catechisms, whereas the *Ten Articles* was a collection of doctrinal statements that outlined core Church doctrines.[3] The two types of documents served different purposes in the life of the Church so that one could not replace the other any more than the *Book of Common Prayer* could replace the *Homilies*. Again, it was sometimes the case that one of the formularies was more up to date than another with regards to Protestant theological developments, but that did not mean that the older were simply replaced by the newer. Although things do become more complicated in the later sixteenth century (when, for example, the national primer and long catechism were merged into one), for the most part, the Henrician, Edwardian and early Elizabethan formularies remained in force until they were either revised or replaced by another formulary *of the same kind*. So the *Bishops' Book* did not replace the *Ten Articles* but the myriad unauthorised late medieval catechisms. Likewise, the replacement for the *Ten Articles* was the *Forty-Two Articles* (via the *Thirteen* and *Forty-Five*). One goal of this handbook is therefore to clear up such category errors by dividing the formularies into their right families.

Each chapter opens with an introduction, which overviews the common traits of the family of formularies under consideration. In some cases different examples of the same type of formulary are quite similar, while in other cases more distinctions are evident. For example, although the *Forty-Five Articles* were modified before becoming the *Forty-Two*, and they, in turn, were twice reworked into the enduring *Thirty-Nine Articles*, the dependence of the last on the first is easy to see and their style remains the same. In contrast, the *Ten Articles* are quite different in form and content from the *Forty-Five* yet they are plainly still a collection of articles.

---

[2] C Hardwick (Rev. F Proctor), *A History of the Articles of Religion*, Third Edition (London: George Bell & Sons, 1876), p 50.

[3] I Green, *The Christian's ABC: Catechisms and Catechizing in England c. 1530–1740* (Oxford: Clarendon Press, 1996) catalogues early modern catechisms and is another most valuable work, but it does not list the *Bishops' Book*, even though it does record its successor, the *King's Book*. In personal communications, Prof. Green has acknowledged this was an oversight.

Following the general introductions, most chapters are then divided into four sections.

The **Specific Descriptions** will give some detail of each particular formulary of the general type. So, for the primers, *King Henry's Primer*, *King Edward's Primer*, and *Queen Elizabeth's Primer* are considered separately, along with other sanctioned primers of the period. While the primary focus of this handbook is on those formularies that can lay some claim to having been officially endorsed, it also gives attention to some other historically important, but unsanctioned, documents. So, for example, although the *Forty-Five Articles* was only ever a working set, it is included for completeness and because of its very direct relationship to the officially approved *Articles of Religion*. Where a non-sanctioned formulary is discussed, its heading is given in square brackets.

While describing the different formularies is straightforward enough in most cases, there are some for which there are no standard or 'type' versions. The *Great Bible* offers perhaps the best example of this, as it went through seven separate and distinguishable printings. Matters are further complicated by the fact that there are some extant 'mixed' copies of the *Great Bible*, which were compiled from quires taken from separate printings, which means that any strict notion of fixed 'editions' is hard to maintain. In cases like these, a single volume is taken as representative of the formulary in question.

A **History** of each family of documents is given next, but this is kept brief as both in-depth, and neatly summarised, histories of most of the documents can be found elsewhere. Key References are provided to encourage deeper investigation.

The sections on **Intended Purpose** will outline—as far as can be determined—the original function and purpose of each formulary, conscious that the uses made of some have changed since the sixteenth century, and that not every document serves the same function in different parts of the Anglican Communion today. For example, it is not at all clear that the *Articles of Religion* were originally intended to function like a comprehensive doctrinal statement, or a confession akin to those of the continental Protestant churches, but there are Anglican Churches today where that role has been constitutionally determined for them. Conversely, volumes such as the primers are essentially absent from today's churches, but they formed a critical part of the doctrinal matrix of the English Reformation. Knowing what purpose each formulary was intended to serve also makes it possible to say what it was *not* originally meant to do. So, again developing a comment made above, if it is known that the *Bishops' Book* was cast as a catechism, it will not be suggested that it was primarily drafted to serve as a preaching script. This may prove important when appealing to the formularies to make historical arguments for or against the place of various doctrines or practices in the Church.

Finally, **Key References** provides a selection of the most important sources of information on each family of documents, often with brief comments added to guide those interested in further research. Two websites are of particular value to anyone wanting to investigate the primary texts of the English Reformation and some of the older, but still invaluable, secondary sources. The first is Early English Books Online at *http://eebo.chadwyck.com*. This is a repository of scanned original documents, although it can only be accessed with a subscription or through a participating library or other institution. The second is *https://archive.org*, which is open access and provides scanned copies of many hard-to-get texts in a range of formats.[4]

A Note on the Scope of this Book

The decision about which dates to put around any period is, to some extent, a historiographical judgement. The period covered by the present volume is bounded by the publication of the *Ten Articles* in 1536 and the convocation in 1571 that finalised the *Thirty-Nine Articles* and the *Second Book of Homilies*. It was during this period that most of the Church's formularies were either created or given their standard form, and then revised to their final, or near-final, form. Some later documents also need to be recognised, such as the *King James Version* of the Bible and the 1604 and 1662 *Books of Common Prayer*. However, these represent relatively minor revisions of earlier formularies and are only better known today because they were the last sanctioned, not because they marked significant developmental steps.

In addition to restricting the timeframe, this guide limits its concern to those works that were part of the Reformation movement. It does not present the works produced by the likes of Papal Legate Reginald Pole

[4] All web links referred to in this book were current as of November 2017.

and Bishop Edmund Bonner under Mary I. In some ways, these works could be slotted neatly into the families of formularies discussed herein—there were articles of religion, injunctions, homilies (including the one Bonner is reputed to have penned for the Edwardian *First Book of Homilies*), and more—but they are tangential to the main lines of development of the Protestant formularies. Certainly, Elizabeth and her Church picked up work on the formularies from where Edward had left off, not from the point to which Mary had taken them. A timeline of the production of the formularies is included as Figure 1.

Figure 1. Timeline of the Production of the Formularies of the English Reformation

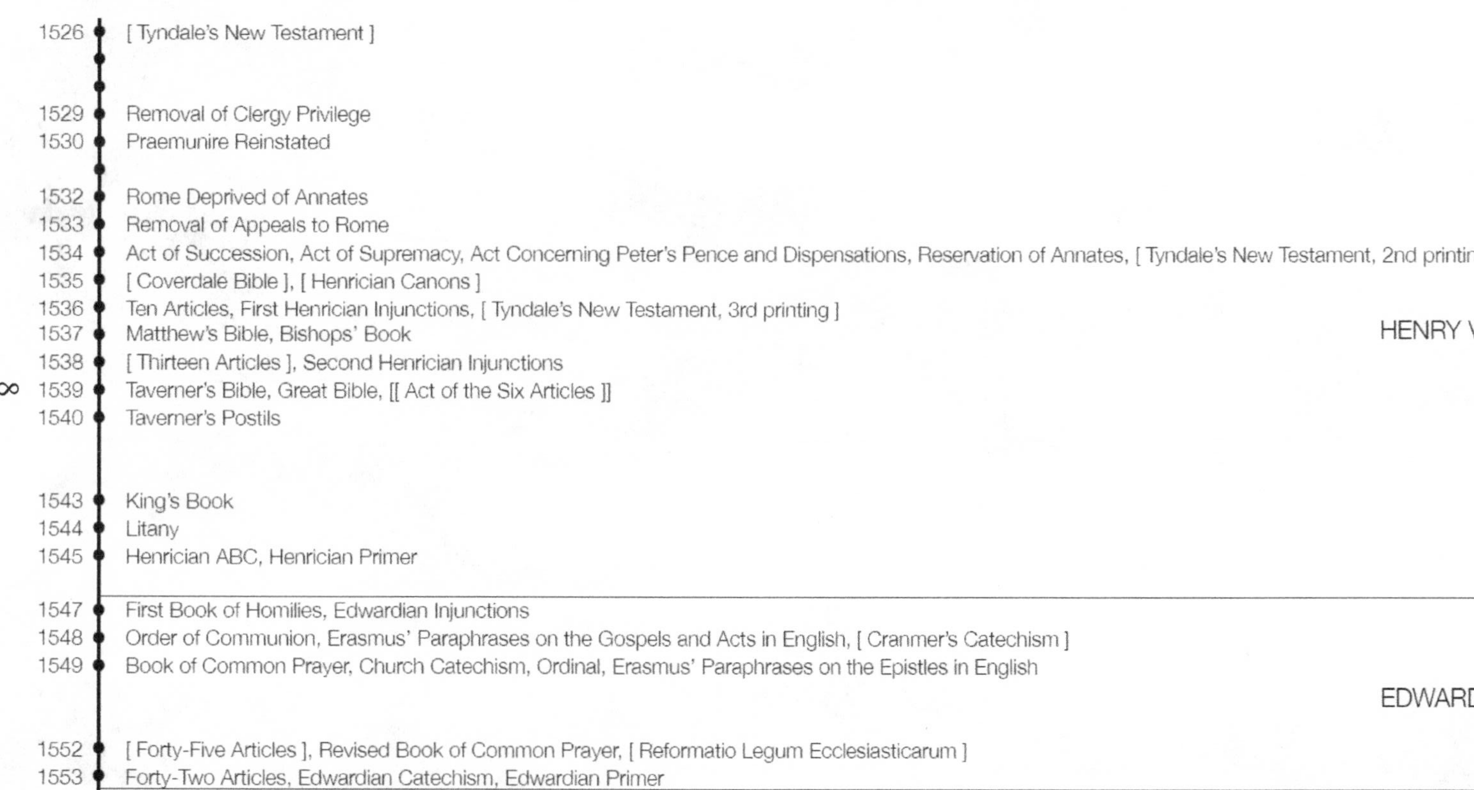

Year	Publications	Reign
1554	[[Marian Injunctions]]	
1555	[[Bonner's Homilies]], [[Marian Primer]]	
1556	[[Pole's Legatine Constitutions]]	MARY I
1559	Revised Book of Common Prayer, Elizabethan Primer, Elizabethan Injunctions	
1560	[Geneva Bible], Orarium	
1563	Thirty-Eight Articles, Second Book of Homilies, [Acts and Monuments in English]	
1564	Preces Privatae	
1568	Bishops' Bible	
1570	Nowell's Full Catechism, Nowell's Middle Catechism, Revised Acts and Monuments in English	ELIZABETH I
1571	Thirty-Nine Articles, Homily Against Disobedience and Rebellion, Canons	
1572	Nowell's Short Catechism	
1576	Revised Acts and Monuments in English	
1578	Book of Christian Prayers	
1583	Revised Acts and Monuments in English	
1604	Revised Book of Common Prayer	
1611	King James Bible	JAMES I / VI
1662	Revised Book of Common Prayer	CHARLES II

[No claim to official sanction]

[[Against the progress of reform]]

1. Articles of Religion

An article of religion is a position statement on an important doctrinal matter. By their very nature, articles are properly theological. In most cases, however, England's official articles do not offer much by way of argued or reasoned theology, but simply assert the view held as orthodox by the Church. All of the official articles of religion are found in collections, the smallest collection comprising ten articles, and the largest, forty-two. Individual articles can be as short as a sentence or as long as a page, but each of the sets run to around ten pages in total. Some of them only exist in Latin, some only in English, and some were prepared in both languages.

Specific Descriptions

The Ten Articles of 1536

This set of articles is explicitly divided into two parts. Its page-long preface explains that the first five articles are expressly commanded of God and necessary for salvation, whereas the second five are not, but are agreeable to Scripture and traditional positions and therefore to be observed for the sake of decent order, unity and polity in churches. The first five articles run to around a page each, although the third on the sacrament of penance is considerably longer, and the second five run to around half a page each. The articles are –

1. Principal Articles Concerning our Faith [i.e. the Bible and creeds]
2. The Sacrament of Baptism
3. The Sacrament of Penance
4. The Sacrament of the Altar
5. Justification
6. Of Images
7. Of Honouring of Saints
8. Of Praying to Saints
9. Of Rites and Ceremonies
10. Of Purgatory

Both the range of topics addressed and their division into the two groups deserve comment. The set's Roman Catholic background is clear: penance remains identified as a sacrament and Articles 6 to 10 are concerned with the cult of the saints and Catholic doctrines of the afterlife. But the inclusion of an article on justification shows the growing priority of this central Protestant doctrine for the English Church in the 1530s. A further shift in tone from medieval Catholicism is seen in the way that rituals associated with the saints and other departed believers are categorised as unnecessary for salvation. The article on purgatory is especially interesting for the degree of uncertainty it introduces around this core Catholic doctrine.

[The Thirteen Articles of 1538]

Most of the *Thirteen Articles* run to around half a page each, although the article on the Eucharist is just two sentences long, which is most interesting, given both the prominence of this doctrine in the Reformation and the fact that these articles were likely prepared in collaboration with Lutheran divines. As in the *Ten Articles*, the article on penitence is several times longer than all of the rest. In addition to the thirteen main articles there are an additional three, which are also relatively long. The articles are –

1. The Unity of God and the Trinity of Persons
2. Original Sin
3. The Two Natures of Christ
4. Justification
5. The Church
6. Baptism
7. The Eucharist
8. Penitence
9. The Use of the Sacraments
10. The Ministers of the Church
11. The Rites of the Church
12. Civil Affairs
13. The Resurrection of the Body and the Last Judgement

A. Private Mass
B. The Veneration of Saints
C. Images

Both the subjects of these articles and their order of presentation reveal that the *Thirteen Articles* laid the ground for the overall content and shape of the later sets of English articles of religion, starting as they do with the doctrine of God, then discussing sin and justification, before moving to the life and praxis of the Church. They are also more clearly concerned with Protestant doctrine than the *Ten Articles*, addressing the particularly Catholic doctrines in the additional three articles rather than in the main set of thirteen.

The Forty-Two Articles of 1553 [and the Forty-Five Articles of 1552]

The significant increase in the number of articles in the Edwardian sets is balanced by the fact that, on average, each article is much shorter. Unlike the sets that preceded them, Archbishop Cranmer's *Forty-Five Articles* were all brief and pithy, the longest being a couple of paragraphs and many running to a mere few sentences. The full list of the original *Forty-Five Articles* is –

1. Faith in the Trinity
2. The Word of God Truly Made to be Man
3. Of the Going Down of Christ into Hell
4. The Resurrection of Christ
5. The Doctrine of Scripture is Sufficient for Salvation
6. The Old Testament is not Rejected
7. Three Symbols [creeds]
8. Original Sin
9. Free Will
10. Grace
11. The Justification of Man
12. Works Before Justification
13. Works of Supererogation
14. No One But Christ is Without Sin
15. Of Sin Against the Holy Spirit
16. What is Blasphemy Against the Holy Spirit
17. Of Predestination and Election
18. Eternal Salvation on in the Name of Jesus Christ
19. The Moral Precepts of the Law Must be Observed
20. The Church
21. The Authority of the Church
22. The Authority of the General Councils
23. Purgatory
24. No One May Minister in Church Unless Called
25. Church must be in Language that is Known
26. The Sacraments
27. Evil Ministers do not Destroy the Effect of Sacraments

28. Baptism
29. The Lord's Supper
30. Transubstantiation
31. The Corporal Presence of Christ in the Eucharist
32. The Sacrament of the Eucharist is not Kept
33. The Single Offering of Christ was Perfect
34. Celibacy is not Enjoined by the Word of God
35. The Excommunicated are to be Avoided
36. Traditions of the Church
37. Homilies
38. Of the Book of Ceremonies of the Church of England
39. Of the Civil Magistrates
40. Christians' Goods are not in Common
41. It is Lawful for Christians to Swear
42. The Resurrection of the Dead has not been Accomplished
43. The Departed Souls are not with the Bodies, nor Idly Sleeping
44. Millenarians
45. Not all are Saved at Length

In this collection, the broad shape of the *Thirteen Articles* is followed, and although they are not explicitly divided into subsets like the *Ten Articles* some groupings can be discerned. The first seven articles place the Church within the bounds of creedal and biblical Christianity as they affirm the historic orthodoxy handed down from the early ecumenical councils and give a clear, high doctrine of Scripture. Articles 8 to 19 focus on matters of salvation, one of the major doctrinal concerns of the Reformation. Articles 20 to 38 deal with the life of the Church, with Articles 26 to 33 addressing the sacraments. Articles 39 to 41 address civil matters, while the final four articles engage with eschatology.

The greater number of articles in this set arises from its incorporation of more articles on fundamental Christian beliefs, such as those concerning the Scriptures, free will and grace, as well as new articles on some of the specific controversies of the period, such as the use of the vernacular in church, the effectiveness of the ministry of 'evil' ministers, the celibacy of the clergy and beliefs about the intermediate state and end times. Many of the articles are negatively framed against wrong belief, not only in opposition to the old errors of the medieval Roman Catholic Church but also now in opposition to the mistakes of more radical contemporaneous reformers, often collectively referred to as 'anabaptists'. Thus these articles reveal a Church that was not only breaking away from its past but also wanting to curb novelty in the interpretation of the faith by unsanctioned theologians and religious leaders of the time.

A further interesting feature of these articles is their endorsement of other formularies of the English Church, namely the *Homilies* and the *Book of Common Prayer*, which shows that they were consciously crafted as part of the closely interrelated web of new theological documents and not as a standalone formulary.

The *Forty-Two Articles* are similar to the *Forty-Five*, the major difference being that the four articles on the Lord's Supper are joined together, unaltered, into a single extended article, which accounts for the set's reduction in number. Other differences between the two sets include the removal of the final sentence of Article 3, on the descent of Christ to hell between his death and resurrection, and some reworking of the articles on original sin and civil magistrates.

When Articles 30 to 32 of the *Forty-Five Articles* were all subsumed into Article 29 of the *Forty-Two*, the numbering of the articles that followed changed. So, for example, Article 33 on the perfection of the single offering of Christ in the *Forty-Five Articles* became Article 30 in the *Forty-Two*, and so on. These types of adjustments continued to be necessary whenever articles were added and removed during a revision—the article above, for example, finally ended up as Article 31 in *The 39 Articles*. It is therefore very important to use a referencing system that avoids confusion when discussing multiple sets of articles. A simple example of such a system is one where individual articles are labelled 'Article *x*/*y*', with *x* being the article number and *y* being the number of articles in the set. Following this, the article discussed above could be referred to as Article 33/45, Article 30/42 or Article 31/39 without any ambiguity.

Thirty-Nine Articles of 1563 and 1571

In overall content and shape, the *Thirty-Nine Articles* are very similar to the *Forty-Two*, although there are some substantial differences between the two sets. Compared with the earlier collection, the *Thirty-Nine Articles* have eight articles removed, five new articles added and many of the retained articles reworked such that, overall, the 1563 *Articles* are around twenty-five percent different to those that preceded them. The bulk of the removals and replacements were of articles relating to salvation and eschatology, and it was Article 29/42 on the Lord's Supper that was the most heavily reworked.

The extent of these changes make it difficult to assert that the *Thirty-Nine Articles* capture a pure Cranmerian theology and, by extension, to claim that the Anglican Church is based on Cranmerian doctrine. This is because the changes to the *Articles* reflect and establish *changes in doctrine*, or at least in doctrinal emphasis, such that the resultant theology of the Elizabethan Church was not identical to Cranmer's but was in some places a development of it, and others a departure from it. England's Settlement theology is not the same as its first Reformation theology. As a rule of thumb, it is not helpful to consider any of the formularies as reflecting or capturing the theology of any individual and many of the efforts to attribute authorship to the formularies are highly speculative. The documents were originally produced by committees and revised by other committees, often with stages of review along the way, and all of the formularies are anonymous, which indicates that they ought to be taken as presenting the theology of the Church at the time, not of any one of its members.

The *Thirty-Nine Articles* underwent a further and final revision in 1571, when an excluded article was restored and a few minor changes of substance were made. Interestingly, the ratification by Queen Elizabeth I is also numbered as the fortieth article in the authorised form.

Table 1 shows the full list of articles included in each of the sets produced between 1552 and 1571.

Table 1. Changes to Articles Included in the *Articles of Religion* between 1552 and 1571

No.		45 (1552; Latin)		42 (1553; Latin)		38 (1563; Latin)		39 (1571)
1	CREEDAL AND BIBLICAL ORTHODOXY	Faith in the Trinity	CREEDAL AND BIBLICAL ORTHODOXY	Faith in the Trinity	CREEDAL AND BIBLICAL ORTHODOXY	Faith in the Trinity	CREEDAL AND BIBLICAL ORTHODOXY	Faith in the Trinity
2		The Word of God was truly made man		The Word of God was truly made man		The Word of God was truly made man		The Word of God was truly made man
3		Of the going down of Christ into Hell		Of the going down of Christ into Hell		Of the going down of Christ into Hell		Of the going down of Christ into Hell
4		The Resurrection of Christ		The Resurrection of Christ		The Resurrection of Christ		The Resurrection of Christ
5		The doctrine of Scripture is sufficient for salvation		The doctrine of Scripture is sufficient for salvation		– *Of the Holy Spirit*		Of the Holy Spirit
6		The Old Testament is not rejected		The Old Testament is not rejected		The doctrine of Scripture is sufficient for salvation		The doctrine of Scripture is sufficient for salvation
7		Three symbols [Creeds]		Three symbols [Creeds]		The Old Testament is not rejected		The Old Testament is not rejected
8	SALVATION	Original sin	SALVATION	Original sin		Three symbols [Creeds]		Three symbols [Creeds]
9		Of free will		Of free will	SALVATION	Original sin	SALVATION	Original sin
10		Of grace		- *Of grace*		Of free will		Of free will
11		Of the justification of man		Of the justification of man		Of the justification of man		Of the justification of man
12		Works before justification		Works before justification		– *Of good works*		Of good works
13		Works of supererogation		Works of supererogation		Works before justification		Works before justification
14		No one but Christ is without sin		No one but Christ is without sin		Works of supererogation		Works of supererogation
15		Of sin against the Holy Spirit		- *Of sin against the Holy Spirit*		No one but Christ is without sin		No one but Christ is without sin
16		What is blasphemy against the Holy Spirit		- *What is blasphemy against the Holy Spirit*		– *Of those fallen after baptism*		Of those fallen after baptism
17		Of Predestination and election		Of Predestination and election		Of Predestination and election		Of Predestination and election
18		Eternal salvation only hoped for in the name of Christ		Eternal salvation only hoped for in the name of Christ		Eternal salvation only hoped for in the name of Christ		Eternal salvation only hoped for in the name of Christ
19		All are bound to the moral precepts of the law		- *All are bound to the moral precepts of the law*	CHURCH	Of the Church	CHURCH	Of the Church
20	CHURCH	Of the Church	CHURCH	Of the Church		Of the authority of the Church		Of the authority of the Church
21		Of the authority of the Church		Of the authority of the Church		The authority of the General Councils		The authority of the General Councils
22		The authority of the General Councils		The authority of the General Councils		Of Purgatory		Of Purgatory
23		Of Purgatory		Of Purgatory		No one may minister in the Church unless called		No one may minister in the Church unless called

No.								
25	SACRAMENTS	Church must be in a language known to the people	SACRAMENTS	Church must be in a language known to the people	SACRAMENTS	Of the Sacraments	SACRAMENTS	Of the Sacraments
26		Of the Sacraments		Of the Sacraments		Evil ministers do not destroy effect of God's institutes		Evil ministers do not destroy effect of God's institutes
27		Evil ministers do not destroy effect of God's institutes		Evil ministers do not destroy effect of God's institutes		Of Baptism		Of Baptism
28		Of Baptism		Of Baptism		Of the Lord's Supper		Of the Lord's Supper
29		Of the Lord's Supper		Of the Lord's Supper		+ *Of both kinds*		++ *The wicked which do not eat the body of Christ*
30		* *Of transubstantiation*		The single offering of Christ on the cross was perfect		The single offering of Christ on the cross was perfect		Of both kinds
31		* *Of the corporal presence of Christ in the Eucharist*	CHURCH	Celibacy is not enjoined by the word of God for any	CHURCH	Celibacy is not enjoined by the word of God for any		The single offering of Christ on the cross was perfect
32		* *The sacrament of the Eucharist is not kept*		The excommunicated are to be avoided		The excommunicated are to be avoided	CHURCH	Celibacy is not enjoined by the word of God for any
33		The single offering of Christ on the cross was perfect		Traditions of the Church		Traditions of the Church		The excommunicated are to be avoided
34	CHURCH	Celibacy is not enjoined by the word of God for any		Homilies		Homilies		Traditions of the Church
35		The excommunicated are to be avoided		- *Of the book of ceremonies of the Church of England*		+ *Of consecration of bishops and ministers*		Homilies
36		Traditions of the Church	CIVICS	Of the Civil Magistrates	CIVICS	Of the Civil Magistrates		Of consecration of bishops and ministers
37		Homilies		Christians' goods are not common		Christians' goods are not common	CIVICS	Of the Civil Magistrates
38		Of the book of ceremonies of the Church of England		It is lawful for Christians to swear		It is lawful for Christians to swear		Christians' goods are not common
39	CIVICS	Of the Civil Magistrates	ESCHATOLOGY	- *Resurrection of the dead has not been accomplished*				It is lawful for Christians to swear
40		Christians' goods are not common		- *Departed souls are not with the bodies, nor sleep idly*				++ *[RATIFICATION]*
41		It is lawful for Christians to swear		- *Millenarians*				
42	ESCHATOLOGY	Resurrection of the dead has not been accomplished		- *Not all are saved at length*				
43		Departed souls are not with the bodies, nor sleep idly						
44		Millenarians						
45		Not all are saved at length						

* These Articles would all be merged, unchanged, into Article 29 of the 1553 Articles.

\- These Articles would be removed from the 1563 Articles.

\+ These Articles were added into the 1563 Articles.

++ This Article and the ratification were introduced in the 1571 Articles (although the article had been proposed in 1563).

In addition to these joinings, deletions and additions, many of the remaining articles were also edited, quite significantly in some cases.

History

The earliest set of English articles was the Henrician *Ten Articles* of 1536. Although it post-dates the close of the Reformation Parliament (1529–1534) when England formally broke with Rome, it cannot be considered a Protestant collection. It is perhaps best thought of as a document very reflective of its time; a formulary with a transitional theology, still partially attached to the old Catholicism yet beginning to embrace the priorities of the Reformation. The individual articles from this set were not carried through into later sets of articles, but its articles on justification and purgatory—which signal a move away from medieval Catholicism—were included as additions to the long catechism, commonly called the *Bishops' Book*, that appeared just one year later (see chapter 4).

In 1538, the *Thirteen Articles* were produced by a meeting of English and German theologians, who together were attempting to formulate a joint statement of beliefs. The project failed and the *Thirteen Articles*, along with the additional three articles, were lost until 1847, when Henry Jenkyns rediscovered them as part of his work compiling Archbishop Thomas Cranmer's writings. The historical importance of the *Thirteen Articles* is that they seem to have been influenced by the *Augsburg Confession* of 1530 or *Wittenberg Articles* of 1536 and therefore may have been a channel through which German theological influence flowed into Cranmer's *Forty-Five Articles*.

Around 1552, after Edward VI had been on the throne for five years, Cranmer presented his *Forty-Five Articles*. These may well have been largely his own personal production, as there is no evidence that he worked on them in committee. Unlike the *Ten Articles* and the *Thirteen Articles*, the *Forty-Five Articles* are a direct precursor to the enduring *Thirty-Nine Articles*, the latter being a revised version of the former.

The first adjustments to the *Forty-Five Articles* took place in 1553, giving rise to the better-known set of *Forty-Two Articles*. The *Forty-Two Articles* seem to have passed through the convocation of Canterbury in 1553 but whether they ever actually came into force is debated point. It is also a moot point, given that Edward died within a few weeks of their appearance—and with him, England's entire programme of reform for the duration of the reign of Mary I. The *Forty-Two Articles* were, however, revived and revised during the reign of Elizabeth I, along with many of the other formularies that had been prepared under Edward. The major revision was conducted as part of the 1563 convocation. Although the broad shape and contents of the *Articles* were preserved through this revision, there were some significant additions, deletions and alterations that affected perhaps one quarter of the substance of the *Articles* and resulted in a set of just thirty-nine.

The changes made during this revision came in at least two waves, with some being made before the convocation by Archbishop Matthew Parker and a small drafting team, and others during the meeting of convocation proper. Then, following the convocation, Queen Elizabeth made an addition to Article 20/39 on the authority of the Church, indicating that it (and thus ultimately herself as its Supreme Governor) held the power to decree its own rites and ceremonies and, significantly, to adjudicate in controversies of faith. Even more controversially, she also removed an article, proposed to follow Article 28/39, which aimed to explain that the wicked, or faithless, do not partake of Christ in the Lord's Supper even though they might consume the bread and wine. For the bishops with a more reforming spirit, the addition of that article had been absolutely essential as a safeguard against any notion of a real carnal presence of Christ in the elements. That interpretation had been made possible for the first time by the very heavy and repeated reworking of Article 28/39 on the Lord's Supper, one of the most fiercely contested doctrines of England's Reformation. It is likely that Elizabeth had the article removed, not because of Roman Catholic sympathies (which the other articles clearly eschew), but because it complicated her attempts at diplomacy with the Germans, whose Lutheran doctrine of the sacrament would have been excluded by it.

In 1571, Bishop John Jewell of Salisbury oversaw the final stage of revision of the *Articles of Religion.* At this point, Article 29/39 on the wicked not eating the body of Christ in the eucharist was able to be returned to its place, something made possible by the fact that an alliance with the Germans had become less of a priority. The other changes made by Jewell were minor and included tidying headings, filling out the list of apocryphal books and adding one title to the list of authorised homilies.

There has been some confusion over the fact this final revision is referred to as the *Articles* of 1562, not of 1571, in both their own preface and the parliamentary act that required subscription to them. This has left a door open for those who want to assent to the Articles of Religion as they were prior to the revision that returned Article 29/39; that is, those in Anglican churches who want to hold to a more Lutheran—or even Catholic—view of the Lord's Supper. But there was never any intention to create such a loophole, nor is any confusion necessary. The 1562 Articles are referred to in the preface and the act simply because the Articles of 1571 were considered to be the same as those of 1562. Jewell's final revisions were not understood to have produced a new set of articles, but only to have finalised the substantial revisory work begun by the convocation eight years earlier.

Intended Purpose

In sixteenth and seventeenth century Europe, leaders of the different Protestant groups invested a great deal of energy into systematising and articulating their beliefs, in many cases over and against the doctrines of Rome. These efforts gave rise to the many denominational 'Confessions'. Examples include the Augsburg Confession (1530), the Helvetic Confessions (1536, 1566), the Gallican Confession (1559) and later the Westminster Confession (1646). At a similar time, the Roman Catholic Church was also reconsidering, reformulating and re-presenting its own doctrines in the Council of Trent (1545–1563) and its canons. But it is not immediately clear that the English *Articles of Religion* constitute a Confession *per se* or any other summary of a comprehensive theological system. Cranmer may have originally intended such a summary with his *Forty-Five Articles*, as they engage with a wide range of doctrines, including grace and eschatology. But even if this is correct, Cranmer's *Articles* are notably cautious, consciously reactionary and situation-specific, with many of them framed negatively against particular beliefs of the Roman Catholics and Protestant radicals.[1] They were intended to locate the Church within the bounds of historical biblical and creedal orthodoxy—an orthodoxy not limited to any one national, or denominational, church—and to make plain where it stood on contested contemporary matters. This purpose is given in the extended title of the original English version of the *Forty-Two Articles*, which says that they were produced –

[1] In the Edwardian *Articles*, the Roman Catholics were referred to as 'School Authors', meaning medieval scholastic theologians. In the Elizabethan *Articles*, the label was changed to 'Romish'.

> for the avoiding of controversy in opinions, and the establishment of a godly concord in *certain matters* of religion.[2]

Moreover, Cranmer's *Articles* were not produced for the general populace, but primarily as a benchmark for the clergy, or 'all suche as shal be admitted to be preachers or ministers in any part of the realme'.[3]

It is similarly difficult to make a case for the Elizabethan *Articles* as a comprehensive confession of faith, as they not only stripped away many of the Cranmerian *Articles* on significant theological matters but also introduced greater ambiguity into some of those they maintained. For example, although there was a call from Bishop Alley of Exeter to clarify interpretation of Article 3/39 on the descent of Christ into hell, the 1563 convocation actually cut the article down so that its final form offered no interpretation of the basic creedal statement on the descent. Similarly, the revisions to Article 28/39 allowed for a much wider range of views on the real presence than Cranmer had. The argument could be made that the Elizabethan divines had intended the *Articles* to be comprehensive in essential doctrine, and had only withdrawn articles or allowed greater ambiguity when doing so better reflected the breadth within orthodox Protestantism. Such an argument would, however, seem to be driven more by the desire to see the *Articles* as a confession of faith than by their contents and the history of their production.

The English *Articles of Religion* never had quite the same place in the life of the Church as the European confessions, due at least in part to the fact that England's Reformation was a top-down, nationwide project. This meant that identification with the Church had more to do with being a subject of the realm than with personal acceptance of its *Articles*. It seems that the purpose of the English *Articles* was first to screen out dissidents from among the clergy and public officeholders of England (who would all be required to publicly assent to them), and second to identify heterodox belief for under-educated clergy who might encounter it in the course of their ministries. Lay people may well have heard the *Articles* read out on occasion—the Preface to the Marian *Eleven Articles* of 1559 required that they be declared in the public worship services

[2] Emphasis added. This titling is not with the *Forty-Five Articles*, but is added to the *Forty-Two*.

[3] Hardwick, *History*, p.73.

twice annually—but it is not clear that many would have been very familiar with them.

Given this, the popular idea that the *Thirty-Nine Articles* were intended to be the universal doctrinal statement of the reformed Church of England is mistaken. While they certainly did have formal sanction at the highest levels, and no variance from their teaching was permitted, their purpose was relatively narrow. Other formularies held equal authority on doctrinal matters and, in fact, if any family of formularies was regarded as the repository of the sum of faith for all of the people, it was the catechisms, not the *Articles*.

It is true, however, that since the Reformation, some of the world's Anglican Churches have adopted the *Thirty-Nine Articles* as one of their fundamental doctrinal standards under the Bible. For example, Canon A5 of the Church of England states that –

> The doctrine of the Church of England is grounded in the Holy Scriptures, and in such teachings of the ancient Fathers and Councils of the Church as are agreeable to the said Scriptures.
>
> In particular such doctrine is to be found in the Thirty-nine Articles of Religion, *The Book of Common Prayer*, and the Ordinal.[4]

And the Ruling Principles of the *Constitution of the Anglican Church of Australia* state –

> This Church, being derived from the Church of England, retains and approves the doctrine and principles of the Church of England embodied in the Book of Common Prayer together with the Form and Manner of Making Ordaining and Consecrating of Bishops, Priests and Deacons and in the Articles of Religion sometimes called the Thirty-nine Articles ... it is hereby further declared, that the above-named Book of Common Prayer, together with the Thirty-nine Articles, be regarded as the authorised standard of worship and doctrine in this Church, and no alteration in or permitted variations

4 https://www.churchofengland.org/more/policy-and-thinking/canons-church-england/section-a.

> from the services or Articles therein contained shall contravene any principle of doctrine or worship laid down in such standard.[5]

This, however, is not the formal or explicit position of every Anglican Church, nor of the Anglican Communion as a whole. The Communion's website says that the doctrinal foundations of the Church are in the Bible, the three creeds, the distinctive ways of Anglican worship found in the *Book of Common Prayer*, doctrinal statements (with the *Thirty-Nine Articles* holding 'a particular historical importance'), other important texts (which is a catch-all category for works such as the *Homilies*, *Hooker's Laws of Ecclesiastical Politie*, the Chicago-Lambeth quadrilateral and the catechisms) and, finally, in 'Continuing Discussion', which is really a forum, not a foundation.[6]

Key References

There are many commentaries and resources for those wanting to study the *Articles* in more depth. This selection presents a range of the most significant titles.

G L Bray (ed.), *Documents of the English Reformation* (Cambridge: James Clarke & Co. Ltd, 1994)

> This volume provides the text of the different sets of *Articles*, apart from the *Forty-Five*, including introductions to each and English translations where the originals are in Latin. It also has the text of the three additional articles found by Jenkyns with the *Thirteen Articles*. Some may find it difficult to follow Bray's style of offering just one main text with the variations signified by different formatting.

G L Bray, *The Faith We Confess: An Exposition of the 39 Articles* (London: The Latimer Trust, 2009)

[5] https://www.anglican.org.au/data/1._The_Constitution_of_the_Anglican_Church_of_Australia-2016.pdf.

[6] http://www.anglicancommunion.org/identity/doctrine/foundations.aspx.

As the title suggests, this volume gives an exposition of the *Thirty-Nine Articles,* recognising them as one of the key repositories of doctrine for the Anglican Communion.

W H Griffith Thomas, *The Principles of Theology: An Introduction to the Thirty-Nine Articles,* fifth edition, revised (London: Church Book Room Press Ltd., 1956)

This is a standard commentary on the *Articles* that is helpful for going through the teaching of each article individually and in some detail.

C Hardwick, *A History of the Articles of Religion,* third edition (London: George Bell and Sons, 1881)

Hardwick offers the best account of the development of the *Articles* and this volume is a standard source for most of the later works on their history. Hardwick has made some mistakes in a few places, but these are minor and will be relatively inconsequential for most studies of the *Articles.* Hardwick includes the text of the different sets of *Articles* in his appendices, and the third edition even has the full text of the *Forty-Five Articles,* which may not be reproduced anywhere else. The manuscript of the *Forty-Five Articles* is held among the Edwardian domestic state papers, SP 10/15/28, in The National Archives in London.

J Lamb, *An Historical Account of the Thirty-Nine Articles from the First Promulgation of them in M.D.LIII. to their Final Establishment in M.D.LXXI* (Cambridge: Deightons, 1829)

This volume is hard to find but useful for anyone wanting to trace the changes made to the *Articles* in the 1563 convocation. Its greatest strength is not Lamb's text, which is minimal, but the fact that it reproduces a typeset version of the manuscript that was worked on during the convocation, including deletions and pen strokes in red ink that follow Archbishop Matthew Parker's red pencil marks in the original. The original manuscript is among the *Synodalia* papers, MS121, held in the Parker Library, Corpus Christi College, Cambridge.

T Rogers, *The Catholic Doctrine of the Church of England, An Exposition of the Thirty-Nine Articles*, ed. JS Perowne (Cambridge: Cambridge University Press, 1854)

This volume is important because of its age, the original (in two parts) dating back to 1585 and 1587. Being such an early commentator on the *Thirty-Nine Articles*, Rogers is able to provide a perspective on their context that is relatively unfiltered by time.

http://prydain.wordpress.com/resources-on-the-thirty-nine-articles-of-religion/

This page lists most of the commentaries on the *Articles* produced up until the early 1900s.

2. Bibles

Each of the authorised English Bibles of the Reformation period had the following in common: they were in the vernacular, printed in blackletter typeface, contained the Apocrypha and were huge and heavy folio tomes.[1] Another distinctive and important, yet frequently overlooked, feature of these Bibles is their inclusion of extensive paratexts—additional printed material that was bound into the same covers as the text of the Scriptures. These paratexts varied widely: some of the Bibles were full of decorative elements such as woodcuts, and others were heavy with educational materials like tables, diagrams, lists, summations, marginal comments and treatises containing all manner of information. Commonly, an epistle dedicatory was included which not only praised the sovereign but also at least hinted at the convictions that had given rise to the production of the Bible. A preface to the reader, which was more straightforward in its claims for the Scriptures and directives for reading, was often also present. There are far too many of these materials to offer even a brief exploration in this short handbook, although a list of the paratexts of each of the authorised Bibles is provided in the following *Specific Descriptions*. At this stage, it is enough to recognise their existence as integral and characteristic parts of the early English printed Bibles.

The Apocrypha was included in the early printed English Bibles as a gathered collection of books placed between the Old and New Testaments. The practice of grouping the Apocrypha in this way had been popularised by Luther and it produced Bibles that were in stark contrast to the Latin *Vulgate* of the Roman Catholic Church which had the Apocryphal books integrated at different points throughout the Old Testament. The contemporary significance, therefore, was not that the Apocrypha was included with the Bible, but that it was separated out from the canonical Scriptures.

---

[1] 'Folio' is the largest format for early printed volumes with each page being around 40 centimetres tall, although sizes varied due to a lack of universal standards. Folio volumes are produced when the printer's paper is folded only once. 'Quarto' volumes are around half the size of folios, the paper having been folded twice (into quarters), and 'octavo' volumes are half the size again, the paper having been folded once more (into eighths).

Specific Descriptions

None of the Bibles discussed in the following pages were originally called by the (now-common) names used here, but instead were simply given titles such as 'The Byble', 'The holi bible' or similar.

[Tyndale's New Testament of 1526, 1534 and 1536]

Tyndale's New Testament was first printed in 1526 as a small, octavo volume, and it was almost completely unadorned. The 1534 printing was the first to see the addition of many paratexts, including the now-famous prologues to all of the individual books (except for Revelation). The 1534 and 1536 editions also contained brief, calendarised Old Testament readings, indicating that these volumes were intended for regular devotional reading as well as private study. By 1536, *Tyndale's New Testament* was also being printed in quarto. Tyndale's translation is famous because it was the first printed English New Testament, because it pioneered the practice of translating English Bibles from the original languages, because it was a risky undertaking at a time when England had not yet fully embraced Protestant values, and because of its controversial translation of some words. The paratexts of the printings of *Tyndale's New Testament* are –

- *1526*
    - To the Reder
    - *Woodcuts* [throughout]
- *1534*
    - W.T. Vnto the Reader [with subsections on Repentaunce and Elders]
    - A prologe into the .iiii. Euangelystes shewynge what they were & their auctoryte
    - A warninge to the reader
    - Willyam Tindale/yet once more to the christen reader
    - The bokes conteyned in the newe Testament
    - A prologe to the Epistle of Paule to the Romayns
    - The Prologe vpon the fyrst epistle of S. Paul to the Corinthyans
    - The Prologe vpon the seconde Epistle of saynct Paul to the Corinthyans
    - The Prologe vpon the epistle of S. Paul to the Galathyans

- The Prologe vpon the epistle of S. Paul to the Ephesians
- The Prologe vpon the epistle of S. Paul to the Philippians
- The Prologe vpon the epistle of S. Paul to the Colossyans
- The Prologe to the fyrst epistle of S. Paul to the Thessalonyans
- The Prologe to the seconde epistle of S. Paul to the Tessalonyans
- The Prologe vpon the fyrst epistle of S. Paule to Timothe
- The Prologe to the seconde epistle of S. Paule vnto Timothe
- The Prologe vnto the pistle of S. Paule to Titus
- The Prologe to the epistle of S. Paul vnto Philemon
- A Prologe to the fyrst epistle of Saynt Peter
- A Prologe to the seconde epistle of S. Peter
- A Prologe vpon the thre epistles of S. John
- The Prologe to the epistle of S. Paul to the Hebrues
- The Prolge vpon the pistles of S. James and Judas
- These are the Epistles taken oute of the olde testament / which are red in the church after the vse of Salsburye vpon certen dayes of the yere [with a subsection, Herafter foloweth the Epistles of the sayntes which are also taken oute of the olde Testament]
- This is the Table/where in you shall fynde / the Epistles and the Gospels / after the vse of Salsbury [with a subsection Here after folowe the Pistles & Gospels of the Saynctes]
- These thinges haue I added to fill vp the leffe with all
- *Marginalia* [throughout]
- *Woodcuts* [throughout, with many large examples in Revelation]

- *1536*

- Willyam Tyndale Vnto the Christen Reader
- The office of all estates
- A prayer to be sayd dayly
- A prologe of S. Matthew
- Marke
- Luke
- John
- A prologe vpon the Epistle of Saynct Paul to the Romayns
- The prologe vpon the fyrst Epistle of Saynct Paul to the Corinthyans
- The prologe vpon the seconde Epistle of Saynct Paul to the Corinthyans

- The prologe vpon the epistle of saynct Paul to the Galathyans
- The prologe vpon the Epistle of S. Paul to the Ephesyans
- The prologe vpon the Epistle of S. Paul to the Philippians
- The prologe vpon the Epistle of S. Paul to the Colossyans
- The prologe vpon the Epistle of S. Paul to the Tessalonyans
- The prologe to the second epistle of S. Paul to the Tessalonyans
- The Prologe vpon the fyrst Epistle of S. Paul vnto Timothe
- The prologe to the second Epistle of S. Paul vnto Timothe
- The Prologe vpon the Epistle of S. Paul to Titus
- The Prologe to the Epistle of S. Paul vnto Philemon
- A prologe to the fyrst Epistle of S. Peter
- The Prologe to the seconde Epistle of S. Peter
- The Prologe vpon the thre Epistles of Saynct John
- The Prologe vpon the Epistle of Saynct Paul to the Hebrues
- The Prolge vpon the Epistles of S. James and Judas
- Here folowe the epistles taken oute of the olde Testament / which are red in the church after the vse of Salsburye vpon certen dayes of the yeare [with a subsection, Here after folowe the Epistles of the Saynctes which are also taken oute of the olde Testament]
- This is the Table wherin ye shall fynde the Epistles and the Gospels / after the vse of Salsbury [with a subsection, Here after folowe the Epistles and Gospels of the Saynctes]
- *Chapter introductions* [throughout the Gospels and Acts]
- *Marginalia* [throughout]
- *Woodcuts* [throughout, with many large examples in Revelation]

[The Coverdale Bible of 1535]

The *Coverdale Bible* was the first complete Bible to be printed in English. It is famous for the beauty of Myles Coverdale's language; Coverdale's Psalter was used in all versions of the *Book of Common Prayer* for this reason. However, despite its pleasing vernacular, this Bible was considered inferior to others by the scholars of the period as it drew from German and Latin translations rather than purely original Greek and Hebrew. The tone of the paratexts in the *Coverdale Bible* is very gentle, with Coverdale expressing a generous stance towards the Apocrypha in his preface to those books. One of the apocryphal books, Baruch, was not separated out from the Old Testament, but held a place between Lamentations and Ezekiel as it had in the *Vulgate*. The paratexts of The *Coverdale Bible* are –

- Because that whan thou goest to study in holy scripture ... [prayers for wisdom, understanding and truth for those reading Scripture]
- An Epistle vnto the Kynges hyghnesse
- A prologe. Myles Coverdale Vnto the Christen reader
- The bokes of the hole Byble
- The translatoure vnto the reader [preface to the Apocrypha]
- *Introductory chapter summaries for each book*
- *Major section title pages*
- *Woodcuts* [throughout]
- *Marginalia* [cross references]

Matthew's Bible (or The Matthew Bible) of 1537

Matthew's Bible was the most staunchly Protestant version produced during the English Reformation. The epistle dedicatory is remarkably bold in the obligation it placed on Henry VIII to allow the reading of the vernacular Scriptures, and several of its other paratexts are cuttingly strong in their criticism of Roman Catholicism. Its Table of Principal Matters—essentially a concise theological dictionary—unashamedly rejects Roman doctrine at several points, the preface to the Apocrypha is very negative about the intertestamental books, and numerous marginal comments throughout reinforce a militant Protestant tone. Much of this material was drawn from the French Protestant Bible of Pierre Robert Olivétan, a relative of Calvin, which highlights a considerable, but often unnoticed, French influence on the early English Bibles.

Also included in *Matthew's Bible*, quite remarkably for the time, was William Tyndale's prologue to the book of Romans. *Matthew's Bible* was, in fact, essentially a compilation of Tyndale's available translations, which accounted for its full New Testament and its Old Testament from Genesis to 2 Chronicles. The remainder of the Old Testament and the Apocrypha were drawn from the *Coverdale Bible* of 1535, with a new translation of the brief apocryphal Prayer of Manasseh added by the compiler. The paratexts of *Matthew's Bible* are –

- These thynges ensuynge are ioyned with thys present volume of the Byble
- The Kalendar
- An Almanack for .xviii. yeares
- An exhortation to the studye of the holy Scripture gathered out of the Byble

- The summe & content of all the holy Scripture / both of the olde and newe testament
- To the moost noble and gracious Prynce Kyng Henry the eyght / kyng of England and of Fraunce / Lorde of Ireland &c. Deender of the faythe ...
- To the Chrysten Readers
- A table of the pryncypall matters contayned in the Byble
- The names of all the bokes of the Byble / and the content of the Chapters of euery book: with the nombre of the leaffe wherin the bokes begynne
- A brief rehersall of the yeares passed sence the begynnynge of the worlde / vnto this yeare of oure Lorde. M.ccccc..xxxvii ...
- To the Reader, [preface to the Apocrypha]
- The Prologe to the Epistle of Saynct Paul to the Romayns
- The is the Table wherein ye shall fynde the Epistles and the Gospels / after the vse of Salisbury
- *Marginalia* [throughout]

Taverner's Bible of 1539

Taverner's Bible is a revised version of *Matthew's Bible*. It offers an improved translation and its paratexts have been edited to make them less combative. The Table of Principal Matters is still present, but the entries most offensive to traditional religion have been either removed or revised. Similarly, the negative preface to the Apocrypha is gone, as is the prologue to Romans, and a new preface to the volume is included. The paratexts of *Taverner's Bible* are –

- To the most noble, most myghtye, and most redoubted prysnte kynge HENRY the VIII, kynge of Englande and of Fraunce, defendout of the fayth, ...
- These thynges ensuynge are ioyned with this present volume of the bible
- An exhortacion to the diligent studye of the holy scripture gathered out of the Bible
- The contentes of all the Holy Scriptvre as well of the olde testament as of the newe
- The names of al the bokes of the Byble, and the content of the Chapters of euery boke

- A brief rehersall of the yeres passed from the begynnge of the worlde, vnto this yere of our Lorde M.D.xxxix. ...
- A table of the principal maters conteyned in the Bible
- This is the Table wherein ye shall fynde the Epistles and the Gospels after the vse of Salisbury
- *Marginalia* [throughout]

The Great Bible of 1539

The *Great Bible* is relatively lacking in paratexts, although from its second edition in 1540, it has carried Cranmer's famous preface calling for carefully controlled Bible reading, which has led to its common identification as 'Cranmer's Bible'. In the margins of some *Great Bibles* there are small text markers, known as 'manicules', indicating where marginal notes were to be added, although they never were. The title page of the *Great Bible* is famously adorned with an impressive woodcut print. It portrays Henry VIII, placed top and centre, passing copies of the Verbum Dei to Archbishop Thomas Cranmer on his right and to Thomas Cromwell, the Vicegerent of the King in Spirituals, on his left. Further down the page, Cranmer and Cromwell are depicted passing the Scriptures onto church and civic leaders, while at the bottom, the people hear them proclaimed and respond with cries of 'Vivat Rex'. (It is somewhat ironic that the woodcut includes so much Latin, given that it celebrates the king's benevolence in distributing Scriptures in English.) The paratexts of the *Great Bible* are –

- The Kalender
- Almanacke for .xviii. yeres
- An exhortacyon to the studye of the holy Scripture gathered out of the Byble
- The summe and content of all the holy Scripture, both of the olde and newe Testament,
- A prologue, expressynge what is meant by certain sygnes and tokens that we haue set in the Byble
- A descripcyon and successe of the kynges of Juda and Jerusalem, declarynge whan & vnder what kynges euery prophet lyued. ...
- A prologue or preface made by the moost reuerende father in God, Thomas Archbyshop of Canturbury Metropolytan and Prymate of Englande [from 1540]

- The names of all the bookes of the Byble / and the content of all the Chapters of euery booke, wyth the nombre of the leaffe where the bookes begynne
- To the Reader [preface to the Apocrypha]
- A Table to fynde the Epistles and Gospels vsually red in the church, after Salysbury vse, where of the first line is the Epistle, & the other the Gospell: ...
- Here followeth the table of the Epistles & Gospels whych are vsed to be red on dyuers saynctes dayes in the yeare
- *Marginalia* [cross references]

[Geneva Bible of 1560]

The *Geneva Bible* is quite different in form to most of the printed English Bibles that had preceded it. Aside from being the best English translation of the Reformation period, it is printed on quarto paper, does not use heavy blackletter typeface, is richly supplied with marginal notes, and is also the first printed English Bible to have its text divided into verses; the previous English Bibles had lettered the paragraphs instead. This is all because, unlike the great lectern Bibles, the *Geneva Bible* was prepared for personal reading, and even personal study. The paratexts of the Geneva Bible are –

- The names and order of all the bookes of the olde and newe Testament with the nombre of their chapters, and the leafe where they begyn
- To the moste vertvovs and noble Qvene Elisabet, Quene of England, France, and Ireland, &c. Your humble subjects of the English Churche at Geneua, ...
- To ovr beloved in the Lord the brethren of England, Scotland, Ireland, &c. Grace, mercie and peace, through Christ Iesus.
- The description of the holie land, conteining the places mentioned in the foure Euangelistes, with other places about the sea coasts, ...
- The description of the covntries and places mencioned in the Actes of the Apostles from Italie on the West parte, vnto the Medes & Persians towardes the East, ...
- A brief table of the interpretation of the propre names which are chiefly founde in the olde Testament, wherin the first nombre signifieth the chapter: ...

- A table of the principal things that are conteined in the Bible, after the order of the alphabet. The first nombre noteth the chapter, and the second the verse.
- A prefite svppvtation of the yeres and times from Adam vnto Christ, proued by the Scriptures, after the collection of diuers autors.
- The order of the yeres from Pauls conuersion shewing the time of his peregrination, & of his Epistles writen to the Churches.
- *Introductory book arguments* [throughout]
- *Introductory chapter arguments* [throughout]
- *Marginalia* [throughout]

The Bishops' Bible of 1568

The *Bishops' Bible* is the most aesthetically elaborate of the early printed English Bibles. It is ornately bound and full of woodcut images, capitals and decorative borders. It contains a great many paratexts, including some devotional and liturgical resources that parallel some of the contents of the *Book of Common Prayer*. Like the *Great Bible*, the title page presents a grand image of the enthroned monarch, now Elizabeth I. The *Bishops' Bible* is the first authorised version to divide the text into verses, following the *Geneva Bible* of 1560. Unfortunately, despite its magnificent production, the translation of the *Bishops' Bible* was not generally regarded as being of the same quality as either its paratexts or its competitors. The paratexts of the *Bishops' Bible* are –

- The summe of the vvhole Scripture, of the bookes of the olde and new Testament
- This table setteth out to the eye the genealogie of Adam, so passing by the Patriarches, Judges, Kinges, Prophtees [sic.], and Priestes, and the fathers of their tyme ...
- The whole scripture of the Bible is deuided into two Testamentes, the olde Testament and the newe, which booke is of diuers natures ...
- A Preface into the Byble folowyng
- A prologue or preface made by Thomas Cranmer, late Archbishop of Canterburie,
- A description of the yeres from the creation of the worlde, vntill this present yere of 1568. drawen for the most part out of the holy Scripture, ...

- Proper lessons to be read for the first lessons both at Morning and Euening prayer, on the Sundayes throughout the year, and for some also the second lessons
- Proper psalmes on certayne dayes
- The order howe the rest of holy scripture beside the Psalter, is appoynted to be read
- A briefe declaration when euery Terme beginneth and endeth
- An Almanacke
- To fynde Easter for euer
- These to be obserued for holy dayes, and none other
- A table for the order of the Psalmes, to be sayde at Morning and Euenyng prayer
- The Kalendar
- The order of the bookes of the olde Testament
- The order of the bookes of the newe Tesetament
- A Prologue of saint Basill the great, vpon the Psalmes
- Numerus secundum Hebreos
- The descripton of the holy lande, conteyning the places mentioned in the foure Euangelistes, with other places about the sea coastes: ...
- A preface into the newe Testament
- The Cart Cosmographie, of the peregraination or iourney of Saint Paul, with the distaunce of the myles
- The order of tymes
- A Table to fynde the Epistles and Gospels read in the Church of Englande, VVhereof, the first lyne in the Epistle, and the other the Gospell: ...
- Here foloweth the table of Epistles and Gospels which are vsed to be read on diuers saintes dayes in the yere
- *Marginalia* [throughout]
- *Introductory chapter arguments* [throughout]
- *Small paratextual additions set within the text, for example –*
    - *At* Genesis 2: a figure showing the location of Eden
    - *At* Exodus 27: a diagrammatic plan of the Israelite camp
    - *At* Leviticus 18: Degrees of kinred, whiche let martimonie ... and Degrees of affinitie or alianunce ...
    - *At* Numbers 33: This Charte sheweth the way that the people of Israel passed the space of fourtie yeres, ...

The King James Version of 1611

Despite having the greatest profile for subsequent generations, the *King James Bible* was the plainest of the early printed English Bibles. It still contained a few paratexts but, apart from the epistles dedicatory and to the reader, these were only of the liturgical type. The bulk of educational materials common to the earlier Bibles was removed. The *King James Bible* paratexts are –

- The Epistle Dedicatory
- The Translators to the Reader
- Calendar
- An Almanack for 39 Years
- Directions to find Easter
- The Order of Psalms and Lessons to be said at Morning and Evening Prayer
- The Names and Order of the Books of the Old and New Testament
- *Marginalia* [cross references]

History

The mass production and wide distribution of vernacular Bibles was one of the great aims and achievements of the Protestant Reformation. The pioneer of English Bible translation in the sixteenth century was William Tyndale, who, being influenced by Martin Luther, produced a New Testament in 1526 after having moved to the continent. Although many copies of Tyndale's work were smuggled into England, it came too early for official acceptance. As recently as 1521, Pope Leo X had given the title 'Fidei Defensor' to Henry VIII for the latter's work *Defence of the Seven Sacraments*, which supported Roman Catholic theology in direct opposition to Luther's challenges. Tyndale's text, on the other hand, was pointedly anti-Roman in its translation of Greek words such such as ἐκκλησία (ekklesia), which he rendered 'congregation' rather than 'church', thereby highlighting the local, not the macro-institutional, nature of the Christian gathering.

Tyndale was also out of favour with Henry for his challenge to the royal divorce, and in 1536, having been betrayed and captured in Antwerp, he was executed. According to the martyrologist John Foxe, Tyndale's dying words were 'Lord! Open the king of England's eyes'. That prayer was answered just one year later with the publication of *Matthew's Bible* carrying the formal privilege of the crown. This turn of events is even more remarkable when it is realised that *Matthew's Bible* was far more Protestant than *Tyndale's New Testament* ever was, and that its text comprised mostly Tyndale's translations anyway.

Henry may have allowed the translation to go forward because his theological position had indeed shifted since his clashes with Tyndale, something which is obvious from the progress of the Reformation Parliament under the direction of Henry's right-hand man Cromwell. But it may be due more to the fact that Tyndale's name was not explicitly attached to *Matthew's Bible*—although his controversial translations remained and there was a large, decorative 'WT' printed at the close of the Old Testament for those with eyes to see it. Perhaps Henry did know that the text was largely Tyndale's, but was satisfied that it was not obviously so, meaning that he would not have had to face any public embarrassment for openly endorsing the work of a recently-executed enemy. Alternatively, Henry may not have been aware that *Matthew's Bible* was largely Tyndale's work under another name. In support of this line of reasoning is the fact that the Bible's compiler, ostensibly 'Thomas Matthew', was really Tyndale's associate, John Rogers, who would later become the first of the Marian martyrs. The use of the pseudonym may have given Rogers the anonymity he needed to make a fresh attempt at presenting Tyndale's translations for authorisation. (It certainly allowed him to pen a preface to Henry that was forthright to the point of being presumptuous. It would not be hard to imagine Henry reacting badly to its tone; if he had done so, the author may well have wished to remain unidentified.) Recognising both the worth of *Matthew's Bible* and the sensitivity of the situation, Cranmer enlisted Cromwell to petition Henry for its acceptance. From their correspondence, we learn that within just nine days Cromwell had been successful.[1]

Not long after this achievement, Cromwell set Richard Taverner to work on a less aggressively Protestant revision of *Matthew's Bible*. The result, now known as *Taverner's Bible*, had only relatively minor changes, but they made it far less theologically provocative. Its publication in 1539 was almost immediately eclipsed by another Bible, this one prepared by Miles Coverdale, also working at Cromwell's direction. Coverdale's work

---

[1] H Jenkyns, *The Remains of Thomas Cranmer, Volume 1* (Oxford: Oxford University Press, 1833), pp 199–202.

progressed his earlier achievement of preparing the first complete English language Bible to have been printed—although it is not clear that that work received the approval of the crown. Because of its size, the 1539 Bible came to be known as the '*Great Bible*', despite the fact that it was not notably larger than the other lectern Bibles of the day. Nonetheless, it also became great in its dominance, effectively rendering all former translations obsolete and remaining uncontested for two decades. Cromwell's Injunctions of 1538 required that a Bible be set up in every church and, in its multiple editions, the *Great Bible* was the version procured by most parishes.

From the second edition in 1540, the *Great Bible* came with a preface written by Cranmer. Around 5,000 words in length, this is primarily concerned with balancing the two priorities of reading the Bible and accepting the approved Protestant interpretation. That is, Cranmer was eager to promote the reading and hearing of the Scriptures, but also to give clear warnings against uncontrolled speculation on their meaning. In this, we see that the English Reformers, like their continental counterparts, were battling not just for the Bible but also for its correct interpretation. In this struggle, Cranmer's preface ultimately proved to be ineffective. In 1543 there was a clampdown on variant interpretations of the Bible with an act of parliament forbidding annotations on the text and restricting commoners from reading the Scriptures. Moreover, Henry stopped the printing of new Bibles and in 1546 ordered that translations other than the *Great Bible* be confiscated and burned.

After this surge of English Bible production, no further authorised version came until Elizabeth I was on the throne. Interestingly, this means that for all the other formularies prepared during his reign, there was no fresh Bible authorised by Edward VI.[2] In order to understand the Elizabethan Bible, it is necessary to consider a version that predated it, the *Geneva Bible* of 1560. As its name suggests, this Bible, although English, was produced on the continent, with labour undertaken by Marian exiles who had fled for fear of persecution. In this context, the translators had different commitments to their predecessors, as well as the freedom to pursue them.

---

[2] In 1549 and 1551 Edmund Becke did prepare revisions of *Matthew's* and *Taverner's Bibles*, infamously known as the 'wife beater' Bibles because of the terrible marginal note at 1 Peter 3:7.

As well as being a new and superior translation, the *Geneva Bible* had a number of distinguishing features. First was its size. Rather than being a giant folio like England's lectern Bibles, the *Geneva Bible* was printed quarto, making it suitable for personal use and for easy concealment if necessary. Second was the fact that it was the first English Bible to have its verses numbered, following the lead set by the Frenchman, Robert Estienne. Versification allowed for quick arrival at specific locations in the text, something that was important if the Bible was not just for devotional reading but also for studying like a textbook. The third distinct feature was its great multiplication of scholia (marginal notes), many of which were drawn from Theodore Beza's *Annotationes* in *Novum Testamentum*. These again aided personal study.

These developments made the *Geneva Bible* widely popular, and this, in turn, drove the leaders of the Elizabethan Church to produce a new and approved alternative that might offer some competition. This was the *Bishops' Bible* of 1568, so named because Archbishop Matthew Parker had apportioned his bishops to oversee the preparation of different sections of the volume. But these episcopal leaders were not scholars of the same calibre as the exiles who had produced the *Geneva Bible*. Additionally, Parker had directed them not to include any marginalia that would serve to resolve controversial issues; his goal was to create a new edition of the Bible that would be broadly acceptable. The result was a version that, while authorised in England, failed to displace the *Geneva Bible* from its place of prominence. The *Bishops' Bible* was also a lectern Bible and so would never satisfy the appetites that had been whetted for more personal access to the Scriptures. Despite a material opulence—which sought to send some clear signals about the glory of the nation—and abundant paratexts exceeding those found in any other early printed English Bible, the *Bishops' Bible* did not appeal to the laity.

It was not until a generation later, at the start of the reign of King James VI of Scotland as James I of England and Ireland, that a new translation, intended to supersede the *Bishops' Bible*, was prepared. The project was initiated in response to the growing disquiet of the English Puritans. As James took up his rule in England, the Puritans had presented him with their Millenary Petition (so called because it was said to have one thousand signatories) outlining their objections to the national state of religion. This precipitated the Hampton Court Conference of 1604 where the decision was taken to produce a new version of the Scriptures. Despite the encouragement coming from the Puritans, the new Bible was produced by committees of clergy who were under instruction to not provide marginalia, controversial translations or anything that would undermine the structure of the English Church. Additionally, the new translation would lean upon earlier English versions, especially the *Bishops' Bible*, and not just on the original languages. The volume was first printed in folio and the traditional paratexts were removed, leaving just a few liturgical resources such as those used in corporate worship services. The *King James Version* was thus primarily envisaged for use in the context of highly-ordered and standardised church services, as authorised Bibles had been since Henry's reign.

Intended Purpose

The *Great Bible's* decorative title page shows the king distributing the word of God to the leaders of the Church and state. What it does not show is the word of God in the hands of the people. Rather, the people receive the word of God via the mouths of the preachers. This image aptly captures what was intended and achieved by the English Reformers. They reclaimed control of the Bible from Rome and they had it distributed throughout the nation. But they did not give it directly to the people for unmediated consideration. This is because the reclamation of the Bible was not only a goal of the English Protestant religious movement, it was also a strategy for furthering Protestant political ambitions, chief among which was the establishment of a nation united in its theological Reformation.

So, while the early English Reformers wanted to liberate and broadly disseminate the teaching of the Bible, they were very clear about what those teachings were and they had little tolerance for alternative readings of the Scriptures. The educative paratexts were clearly provided for the purpose of establishing conformity to the new theological system as much as they were to help guide independent Scriptural exploration. The various prefaces to the reader highlight this well, with many containing explicit directions about the right way to read the Bibles and stern warnings about misreading. That the early authorised Bibles were produced in formats only suitable for church lecterns further underscores the point: the Bibles were to be read primarily in the controlled environment of the church services, not in private homes. One of the reasons that *Tyndale's New Testament* and the *Geneva Bible* were viewed with suspicion by the government was because they came printed in quarto or octavo, making them small, cheap and far more user-friendly for those interested in personal reading and reflection.

As important as it is to recognise the limits and controls placed around Bible reading in the mid-sixteenth century, it would be imbalanced not to view these in the context of the bigger developments. For the first time, the Bible had come to the people in their own tongue. And it was not only permitted to be read in public, it was mandated that almost the entirety of the Bible would be read aloud in every parish church over the course of every year (see the notes regarding the Lectionaries in chapter 3). Given that England was a Christian nation whose populace was expected to be attending church regularly, this was a significant advance in the mass communication of the word of God. While the paratexts could be considered negatively as instruments of indoctrination, they can equally be understood as resources that protected the readers of the Bible from error. Indeed, while some of them have clear agendas, many are objectively educational. It would be wrong to imagine that those who prepared the paratexts and prefaces were only interested in exerting control over the people. Their pastoral approach must also be recognised, as they considered what would best serve the needs of the flock under their care.

Key References

Since the 400th anniversary of the *King James Version* in 2011, books on the English language Bible have proliferated, adding to the substantial number that were already in circulation. Below is a selection that ought to cover most interests in the early printed English Bibles.

The Matthew's Bible, 1537 Edition (Peabody, Massachusetts: Hendrickson Publishers, Inc., 2009)

This beautiful facsimile of the *Matthew's Bible* not only gives readers access to the text but also provides the chance to see it as it was originally presented. It is in a slightly smaller format than the original full folio version.

G L Bray, *Translating the Bible: From William Tyndale to King James* (London: The Latimer Trust, 2010)

This volume offers brief introductions to many English versions of the sixteenth century as well as to the *King James Version*, but its great value is due to its reprinting of their prefaces. It does not include *Matthew's* or *Taverner's Bibles.*

H Cotton, *A List of the Editions of the Bible and Parts Thereof in English, from the Year MDV. to MDCCCXX* (Oxford: Clarendon Press, 1821)

This is a catalogue of the known extant copies of English Bibles produced in the period 1526–1820 (despite the fact that the title indicates 1505–1820). In addition to the list, the appendices contain descriptions of the contents of a great many of the Bibles, akin to the lists of paratexts given above.

D Daniell, *The Bible in English* (New Haven & London: Yale University Press, 2003)

This is a solid work giving a relatively full outline of the history of the English Bibles.

J F Mozley, *Coverdale and his Bibles* (London: Lutterworth Press, 1953)

The focus of this book allows it to offer more depth than most on the Bibles that were produced during the reign of Henry VIII.

V Tsygankova, *Representing the Church & State: Paratexts of the 'Queen Elizabeth Bible'* (Honours Dissertation, University of Pennsylvania, 2011)

This thesis investigates how the decoration of the *Bishops' Bible* reinforced its authority. It is a useful introduction to thinking about the non-verbal messages of the early printed English Bibles. It is available online at:

http://repository.upenn.edu/cgi/viewcontent.cgi?article=1012&context=uhf_2011

V Westbrook, *Long Travail and Great Paynes: A Politics of Reformation Revision* (London: Kulwer Academic Publishers, 2001)

Westbrook's volume is invaluable for the attention it gives to the lesser-known Bibles. For example, she includes whole chapters on *Matthew's* and *Taverner's Bibles.* Although her attention does turn to the minor details of translation, Westbrook also fills out much of the history of the development of these Bibles and makes fresh observations on them.

3. Books of Common Prayer

The most well-known of all the Anglican documents, the *Books of Common Prayer* (*BCPs*) are effectively collections of running sheets for a broad variety of church services, with some supplementary materials included. Those supplementary materials are short essays explaining the rationale of the book, materials for determining moving liturgical dates and the Scriptures for regular services (calendars and tables), and prayers and readings to be included in the services (collects, Gospels and epistles). The outlines themselves contain the words to be spoken aloud during the service by both the clergy and the laity, as well as section headings and instructions for the conduct of the service, known as rubrics.

The services included in the *BCPs* can be divided into two types: the regular congregational services and the occasional pastoral services. The former type includes Morning and Evening Prayer and Holy Communion, while the latter includes the services for baptism, marriage and burial, as well as services for times of particular need, such as during illness. Also in the occasional services are some that can only be conducted by a bishop, those being Confirmation and the different types of ordinations.

Characteristic of the *BCPs* is the heavy use of Scripture throughout. There are many direct quotations of the Bible, both brief and extensive, as well as many allusions to Scripture woven through the prose. The different services of the *BCP* also seek to prioritise the Protestant theological paradigms, emphasising such things as human sinfulness, Christ's sacrifice, repentance and forgiveness, and the services are structured to highlight the shape of gospel life.

The importance of the calendars and tables in the *BCPs* often goes unrecognised. These were radically different from those that preceded them in two related ways. First, they contain very few saints' and feast days. Many of the earlier church calendars were dominated by these commemorations, and consequently shaped church services around them (see chapter 5 for the impact on preaching). Second, in place of those commemorative days the *BCP* calendars offer a program for reading through almost the entire Bible in a year (the Old Testament once, the New Testament three times and the Psalms monthly) in the Morning and Evening Prayer services. The provision of these calendars is thus consistent with the idea that the regular congregational services of the *BCP* serve as vehicles for the delivery of the Bible to the people.

Specific Descriptions

In overall shape and content, the *BCPs* are all quite similar; only on closer inspection do the differences between the versions become clear. Offered here is a survey of some of the major distinguishing features.

The 1549 Book of Common Prayer

This *BCP* is most distinct from the others. Its obvious characteristics are its lack of the *Ordinal* in the early printings (the *Ordinal* not being included until 1550) and its mixed theology. The latter is perhaps most apparent in the prayers for the dead found in the Holy Communion and Burial services. The Holy Communion service is also distinct in its lack of the Ten Commandments, the ordering of its constituent parts, the markers in the text signifying the point at which the priest should pick up the elements, and its words of administration, which are –

> The body of our Lorde Jesus Christe whiche was geven for thee, preserve thy bodye and soule unto everlasting lyfe.
>
> The bloud of our Lorde Jesus Christe which was shed for thee, preserve thy bodye and soule unto everlastyng lyfe.

The contents of the first *BCP* are –

- Preface
- Table and Calendar, with instructions for use
- Matins
- Evensong
- Introits, Collects, Epistles and Gospels
- Holy Communion
- Litany and Suffrages [not in the earliest printings]
- Baptism
- Confirmation
- Matrimony
- Visitation of the Sick
- Communion of the Sick
- Burial
- Purification of Women
- First day of Lent (or Commination against Sinners)

- Of Ceremonies
- Certain notes
- Ordinal [from 1550]

The 1552 Book of Common Prayer

The second *BCP* differs in several important ways from the first, reflecting the fact that this book was the product of the most significant of all *BCP* revisions. In Holy Communion, the entire service has been significantly reordered. The former 'canon', or central prayer of the earlier forms of the service, is divided into three parts, which are then separated by other components of the service, and the act of communion itself is placed immediately after the prayer of consecration. The Ten Commandments have been added to the service and the words of administration have also been changed to –

> Take and eate this, in remembraunce that Christ dyed for thee, and feede on him in thy hearte by faythe, with thankesgeving.
>
> Drinke this in remembraunce that Christ's bloude was shed for thee, and be thankefull.

These changes better reflect the Protestant understanding of the gospel, as do the facts that the invocation of the Holy Spirit and the prayers for the dead have been removed. The whole service now flows down from a prayer for the Church Militant, that is, the living people of God here on earth.

Added at the end of the Holy Communion is the misnamed 'black rubric' or Declaration on Kneeling, which is a statement inspired by John Knox explaining that kneeling during communion is an acceptable way of expressing humble thanks as a recipient of the benefits of Christ's sacrifice, but it is not an act of adoration of the elements as it had been in Catholic times. The Declaration was a late addition to this *BCP* and does not appear in all printings, nor is it always in exactly the same place when it is present.

Other ways that the second *BCP* differs from the first include the renaming of Matins and Evensong to Morning Prayer and Evening Prayer respectively (although not in the calendars), the inclusion of a call to repentance in Morning Prayer, the separation of Proper Psalms and Lessons from Collects, Epistles and Gospels, the removal of the exorcism from Baptism and the moving of the entirety of that service to the front of the church (part had formerly been conducted at the door), the removal of the references to the Apocryphal book Tobit in Matrimony, the separation of Visitation of the Sick and Communion for the Sick, the Purification of Women changed to Thanksgiving for Women After Childbirth, and the removal of the prayers for the dead from the Burial service, a service which was heavily reworked. There has been some minor reordering of the contents including, the essay Of Ceremonies, being moved to the start of the book. It is joined there by the following new materials –

- The ordre howe the Psalter is appointed to be read.
- The Table for the order of the Psalmes to be sayd at Mornyng and Evening prayer.
- The order how the rest of holy Scripture is appointed to be read.
- An Almanack.

The 1559 Book of Common Prayer

Elizabeth I's *BCP* is essentially the same as the 1552 *BCP*, with just a few changes of significance made. The Kalendar has some additional saints' days, although still not as many as were present in the old Catholic calendars. In Holy Communion, the words of administration are a combination of the words from both the 1549 and 1552 *BCPs*, and the Declaration on Kneeling has been removed. In Morning Prayer, contentious additions have been made to the Ornaments rubric, prayers for the sovereign have been added and, in the Litany, the prayers against the pope have been removed. The new Act of Uniformity now opens the book. Oftentimes, Certain Godly Prayers are appended in a collection at the end.

The 1560 Latin Book of Common Prayer

This is a Latin translation of the 1559 *BCP*, and aside from being in the language of scholarship rather than the common tongue, this version includes many more saints' days in the calendar and makes provision for communion in the Burial service, as had also been the case in 1549.

The 1604 Book of Common Prayer

This is a rare volume but has only small differences to the 1559 *BCP*. These include the possibility of forgiveness being declared, rather than granted, in Morning and Evening Prayer, James' Proclamation on

Uniformity, and the addition of the questions on sacraments in the catechism within the Confirmation service.

The 1662 Book of Common Prayer

A great number of minor changes are found in the 1662 *BCP* compared to the 1559 *BCP*. And since its first issue it has undergone countless printings, which have often introduced still more changes to the overall package of resources. In the first printings of the 1662 *BCP*, some of the major additions include –

- A new Act of Uniformity
- Bishop Sanderson's Preface
- The Athanasian Creed
- The Order of Baptism for Those of Riper Years [largely used in missional contexts]
- The Order of Prayers to be Used at Sea
- Forms of Prayer for the Anniversary of the day of the Accession of the Reigning Sovereign
- Articles of Religion
- A Table of Kindred and Affinity.

Also returned to the book are the more Protestant 'black rubric' and the more Catholic directions for manual acts in the Prayer of Consecration in the Communion. Other rubrics are also added to the Communion to address matters such as the need to consecrate additional bread and wine during the service, the practice of covering the elements and the disposal of any remainders of the elements. Other more major changes to this final *BCP* include its use of the *King James Version* of the Bible throughout, the separation of the Catechism from Confirmation (a significant novelty) and removal of the requirement for Communion in Matrimony.

History

Archbishop Thomas Cranmer was the lead complier of the first *BCP*, and it is well known that he drew on a number of pre-existing sources for this work. Less well known, however, is the range of those sources. Following Thomas Drury's neat categorisation,[1] the sources are –

1. Pre-Reformation Sources –

    a. Medieval English services—especially those of the Sarum Rites, which themselves appear to draw on earlier liturgies going back to the fifth century Gelasian Sacramentary.

    b. Early Eastern and Gallican sources—including the Prayer of St Chrysostom and the Mozarabic, or Spanish, Rite.

2. Reformation Sources

    a. Foreign Compositions—notably, Cardinal Quiñones' Breviary, and Archbishop Hermann's Consultation, which was prepared by Martin Bucer and Philip Melanchthon. (Bucer's Censura was also very important during the first revision to the BCP.)

    b. Compositions of English Reformers—Cranmer himself being the foremost.

Perhaps the most heavily used source was the Sarum Rites, and it is possible to think of the *BCP* as its successor, although with a much wider circulation and mandate. The 'Sarum Rites' or 'Sarum Use' is really a collective term for a number of different service books that had been established for regular use at Salisbury. Those books are –

- The Missal—the order for Holy Communion
- The Manual—which contains the occasional, pastoral services
- The Breviary—the 'brief' version of the canonical hours (for which, see chapter 7 on the Primers)
- The Processional—as its name suggests, this was the collection of processional services, of which the Litany was one
- The Pontifical—services that can only be conducted by a bishop
- The Pie—the rulebook, explaining how to put the various liturgical services together

Cranmer's first work towards revising, combining and condensing all of this material was not the *BCP* but his revision of the calendars in the late 1530s. In this he followed the lead of Cardinal Quiñones, who had been

[1] T W Drury, *How We Got Our Prayer Book* (London: Nisbet & Co. Ltd., 1901), p.6.

progressing a similar project for Rome. The importance of Cranmer's calendars in changing the nature of Matins and Evensong—and therefore of a great deal of the purpose and experience of public worship—cannot be overstated. With the inclusion of the calendars in the *BCP*, seriatim Bible reading became the core of the daily church services.

In 1544, at the direction of Henry VIII, Cranmer produced a Litany to be used as a uniform rite across all the realms as a way of seeking God's favour for the upcoming harvest. This was followed in 1548 by a stand alone order for Holy Communion, which was most remarkable, not only for being in English, but also for directing that the laity be given both the bread and wine, something that had not been standard practice in medieval times. Along with the short catechism that appeared in *Henry's ABC* of 1545, these early productions were brought together, along with all of the other service orders and supplementary materials, into the first *BCP* of 1549. In 1550, the *Ordinal* (on which see chapter 6) was added.

While this first *BCP* marked a monumental achievement, many felt that it did not advance Protestant convictions far enough or clearly enough. It was not only that those with a reforming spirit felt uncomfortable at the lingering Catholic theology found particularly in the Communion service and the prayers for the dead, but also that traditionalists, Bishop Stephen Gardiner being chief among them, devised ways of interpreting this *BCP* that were quite harmonious with unreformed doctrine. Martin Bucer, then resident in England as Regius Professor of Divinity at Cambridge, produced his *Censura* to outline his many concerns with the book, and when the major revision of 1552 was complete, around half of his recommendations had been adopted. The resultant second *BCP* was the most unambiguously Protestant of all the editions. It was, however, short lived, as Edward VI's death in 1553 brought Mary I to the throne, whereupon she returned the Church to Rome and its theology.

When Elizabeth became Queen in 1559, the pendulum swung back towards Protestantism, although not as far as it had been under Edward. Nonetheless, Elizabeth again took the 1552 *BCP*—and decisively not the 1549 *BCP*—as the national standard. A number of changes were made at this time, the aim of which appears to have been to bring accord between the Protestants, whose leading lights were returning from their exile on the continent, and the conservatives now placed by Mary in most of the Church's important offices. This conciliatory path is sometimes mistakenly understood as an all-round compromise, which left the

Church in a no-man's land between pure Protestantism and traditional Catholicism, but this is not accurate. Although it is clear that Elizabeth was more open to a breadth of theological interpretation than Edward, it is also plain that she made concessions to the Catholics mostly in matters of form, while in doctrine she frequently adopted the Protestant position.

By the time James became King of England, the Puritan movement had significantly enlarged. The Puritans presented their Millenary Petition in which they outlined their objections to the *BCP*, all of which were in line with their belief that it was not a fully Protestant work. In 1604, James hosted the Hampton Court Conference at which leading Puritans discussed their concerns with a number of James' bishops. Few concessions resulted however, and the 1604 *BCP* is not substantially different from its predecessor. The only notable outcome of the Hampton Court Conference that pleased the Puritans was a commitment to the revision of the *Bishops' Bible*, which led to the *King James Version* of 1611.

The final version of the *BCP* was not produced until 1662, but two other books that had some bearing upon it appeared in the mid 1600s: the *Scottish Book of Common Prayer* of 1637 and the *Directory of Public Worship* of 1645. The *Scottish BCP* contributed a range of minor changes to the 1662 *BCP*, including the return of rubrics for manual acts in the Holy Communion service, the addition of a doxology from Matthew's Gospel to the Lord's Prayer, and the prayers at the end of Morning and Evening Prayer. The *Directory* replaced the *BCP* when the latter was suppressed by parliament at the beginning of the Interregnum. Although it was not made up of orders of services like the *BCP*, the *Directory* did end up contributing the service of prayers for those at sea to the 1662 book. It was as part of the Restoration following the Interregnum that the *BCP* was re-established as the liturgical standard for England and it was in the lead up to this return to usage that the final revisions were made. Bishop John Cosin of Durham was one of the leading hands in this last revision, and his notes are extant in the volume now known as the *Durham Book*, an annotated 1604 *BCP*.

At this time, it was Presbyterians, rather than Puritans, who sought changes, but their requests were again all expressions of a desire for a liturgy that was more fully reformed and that contained less Catholic residue. Negotiations between leading Presbyterians, including Richard Baxter, and bishops, including Cosin, took place at the Savoy Conference of 1661, but resulted in few concessions being made, largely because the Presbyterians were unable to demonstrate the fundamental wrongness of anything in the existing *BCP*. The volume that was finally produced in 1662 remains the standard *BCP* for the entire global Anglican Communion, although many provinces also use authorised supplementary liturgies.

Intended Purpose

It is very easy to discover the intended purposes of the *BCP*, given that these are made explicit in the preface to the 1549 book. That preface explains that the *BCP* was prepared in order to deal with a number of significant problems that existed in the old liturgies. These problems are detailed in Table 2, along with the responsive goals of the *BCP* and the means by which those goals were achieved.

Table 2. Issues Addressed by the *Book of Common Prayer*

Problem	Object of the *Book of Common Prayer*	Means by which the object was achieved
Decline of the ancient tradition of seriatim reading of the whole Bible	Restore focused, systematic reading of the whole Bible in church services	Inclusion of the new calendars and the removal of many disruptive parts of the services
Services conducted in a language the people could not understand	Provide offices that were intelligible and therefore edifying	Provision of the entire *BCP* in English
Rules to run the services overly complicated	Make planning the services a less consuming task than running them	Provision of a much simplified set of rules and clear rubrics
Some false, uncertain and superstitious things included in the services	Purify the doctrines of corporate worship	Removal of all that was not grounded in the Bible
Each parish incurred significant cost in supplying the necessary liturgical resources	Reduce the financial burden on parishes	Compilation of everything required for divine service into a single volume *BCP* plus the Bible

A number of different versions of the services existed across the dioceses of England	Bring national uniformity in worship, and therefore in doctrine	The *BCP* made the sole national standard

Some of the most famous quotations from the *BCP* are found in this preface and concern the problems of the medieval services. They include –

> THERE was never any thing by the wit of man so well devised, or so surely established, which (in continuance of time) hath not been corrupted ...
>
> commonly when any boke of the Bible was began: before three or foure Chapiters were read out, all the rest were unread
>
> many times, there was more busines to fynd out what should be read, then to read it when it was faunde out

Although it has been retitled 'Concerning the Service of the Church', the 1549 preface has remained in all subsequent *BCPs*, where it continues to reiterate its purpose. A new preface was added in 1662, but this differs from the first in that it does not lay out the purposes for which the *BCP* as a whole was promulgated, but rather gives a defence and explanation of the revisions made. It elucidates three purposes that drove those changes. The first was to preserve peace and unity in the Church, the second was to procure reverence and to excite piety and devotion in the public worship of God, and the third was to cut off any opportunity for those who wish to argue against the liturgy. No doubt all the revisions to the *BCP* were similarly motivated.

It is important to recognise that, while the services contained in the *BCPs* were intended for recurring local usage, there were many additional 'special' services for particular times that were authorised by the highest levels of the Church leadership, and these could be mandated for use across the realms. They included services for prayer in times of plague, drought or fear of foreign military powers, thanksgivings for military victories, processions for the health of the royal family and more besides. In some cases, entire liturgies were produced for these services; in others, only extra prayers were supplied for use in conjunction with the established *BCP* services. Recognising the existence of these services makes it clear that the purpose of the *BCP* was not to supply *every* liturgical resource that local churches would ever need, but rather to supply those resources that would be in regular use.

It is similarly necessary to realise that some of the orders in the *BCP* regularly had additional materials spliced into them. Most commonly included were prayers for the Church, for those in various positions of power, and also prayers for the dead as mandated by the various orders for the Bidding of the Bedes. 'Bidding of the Bedes' means 'praying of the prayers', with 'bid' being the Anglo-Saxon word for 'pray'. These prayers were to be said in the service at the time of the sermon or homily and the practice followed on from the old Catholic Prone, which was a part of the service attached to the Mass. Other local concerns were most likely addressed along with the Bidding of the Bedes, such as the reading of the banns for those intending to get married. The Edwardian and Elizabethan versions of the Bidding of the Bedes are found at the close of their respective Royal Injunctions.

Although it remains a unifying document, the *BCP* cannot suffice for every church and diocese in the worldwide Anglican Communion, simply because the *BCP* is a quintessentially English liturgy and the majority of today's Anglicans no longer have English as their first language. The churches in Tanzania naturally and rightly need indigenised Tanzanian liturgies in local languages, just as the churches in India need indigenised Indian liturgies in the local languages. Indeed, there is a very real sense in which the idea of the 'Church of England in Tanzania' or the 'Church of England in India' is an oddity, and this is doubly so in the postcolonial era. In the sixteenth century, the Church of England's primary argument for existence independent of the Roman Catholic Church was based on the doctrine of the Divine Right of Kings, which asserted that each prince was head of both the temporal and spiritual affairs of their own realms. The subsequent internationalisation of what is a fundamentally national Church is, therefore, a development on the Church of England's own Reformation heritage, and it has led to a far more diverse global Communion, one that must account for people of many different cultures and languages and that will require many indigenous liturgies.

Key References

F E Brightman, *The English Rite, Volumes 1 & 2* (London: Rivingtons, 1921)

These volumes are indispensable for anyone wanting to do side-by-side comparisons of the different *BCPs* or for anyone wanting to look back into the sources of the first book, as Brightman has everything laid out in parallel columns. The books also contain informative descriptive and historical information.

M Burkill, *Dearly Beloved: Building God's People Through Morning and Evening Prayer* (London: The Latimer Trust, 2012)

Burkill helpfully explores the intended biblical focus of Morning and Evening Prayer and documents some of the history of these services, both prior to and post 1662.

H O Coxe, *Form of Bidding Prayer* (Oxford: Oxford University Press, 1840)

This is a volume worth consulting for more detail and description of the Bidding of the Bedes.

G J Cuming, *The Godly Order: Texts and Studies Relating to the Book of Common Prayer* (London: SPCK, 1983), chapter 1

Cuming's chapter is a solid investigation of Cranmer's early work in revising the lectionaries that ultimately resulted in the calendar of the 1549 *BCP*.

T W Drury, *How We Got Our Prayer Book* (London: Nisbet & Co. Ltd., 1901)

The beauty of Drury's book is its brevity. In just 124 pages he outlines the history of the different *BCPs* and catalogues the changes made at each stage of revision. In an appendix, Drury gives a full list of these changes.

C Hefling and V Shattuck (eds), *The Oxford Guide to the Book of Common Prayer* (Oxford: Oxford University Press, 2006)

While just Part 1 of this volume addresses the production of the *BCP*, the remainder of the volume is valuable for the breadth of topics related to the liturgies it tackles. Part 6 addresses the different services in the *BCP*.

J Ketley (ed.), *The Two Liturgies, with other Documents set forth by Authority in the Reign of King Edward VI* (Cambridge: Cambridge University Press, 1844)

Ketley's volume is a standard edition of the first two *BCPs*.

N Mears, A Raffe, S Taylor, P Williamson and L Bates (eds), *National Prayers: Special Worship Since the Reformation*, Volume 1: Special Prayers, Fasts and Thanksgivings in the British Isles, 1533–1688 (Woodbridge: The Boydell Press, 2013)

This volume presents a substantial investigation into the other liturgies that were sanctioned for particular uses alongside those in the *BCPs*. It contains both a solid general introduction to those liturgies, as well as a catalogue and description of many, and includes a great volume of newly transcribed material.

C Neil and J M Willoughby (eds), *The Tutorial Prayer Book* (London: Church Book Room Press Ltd., 1959)

This volume offers a thoroughgoing commentary on the contents of the *BCP*, including the *Ordinal* and *Articles*, and includes detail of changes made at each revision.

T Patrick, 'Thomas Cranmer and the Reform of Liturgy' in C Bale, E Loane and M Thompson (eds), *Celebrating the Reformation* (Leicester: Inter-Varsity Press, 2017)

This chapter entails a discussion of the centrality of the lectionaries to Cranmer's work in producing the *BCP*.

F Proctor and W H Frere, *A New History of the Book of Common Prayer* (London: Macmillan & Co Ltd., 1965)

This volume has similar objectives as Drury's, but is far more detailed and comprehensive in its documentation. Part One gives the history of the *BCPs*, and Part Two presents the sources and rationale for each of the offices.

N Scotland, *The Supper: Cranmer and Communion* (London: The Latimer Trust, 2013)

This is a helpful historical, theological and practical examination of the service of the Lord's Supper in the 1662 *Book of Common Prayer.*

B Sargent, *Day By Day: The Rhythm of the Bible in the Book of Common Prayer* (London: The Latimer Trust, 2012)

Sargent offers a thoughtful assessment of the Church calendar, the prayers and texts that feed into it and their importance in nurturing Christian experience.

E C Whitaker, *Martin Bucer and The Book of Common Prayer* (Great Wakering: Mayhew-McCrimmon, 1974)

Whitaker's volume presents a standard English translation of Bucer's *Censura,* which was the stimulus and source for many of the changes made during the first revision to the *BCP.*

http://justus.anglican.org/resources/bcp/england.htm

This website is a fantastic repository of the different editions and printings of the *BCP* and also of some of the modern liturgical revisions.

4. Catechisms

At the core of the catechisms of the English Reformation is the presentation of three brief formulations that together are considered to capture the central and essential matters of the Christian faith: The Apostles' Creed, the Ten Commandments and the Lord's Prayer.

Despite this common focus, the catechisms vary significantly in their contents and length. The shorter ones contain bare-bones presentations of the three formulations and can be printed on a few small leaves of paper. In some cases the shortest catechisms were printed along with an official alphabet, indicative of their connection to the Church's literacy programs. The longer versions dissect and discuss each part of the formulations in considerable detail, often including lengthy digressions into wider theological conversations; consequently, they can fill books of several hundred pages.

In addition to the core triad of materials, many of the catechisms also address other subjects and traditional formulations of the Church. These include the Ave Maria, the doctrines of justification and purgatory or, more standardly in the later years of the Reformation, sacramental theology. Again, different catechisms treat this supplementary material at different lengths.

In terms of format, the catechisms were often presented as interrogatory dialogues between a 'master' and a 'scholar', the former quizzing the latter over their knowledge of the contents and meaning of the three formulations and any other materials.

Specific Descriptions

[The Institution of a Christian Man (commonly known as the Bishops' Book) of 1537]

This long catechism addressed the Apostle's Creed, the Ten Commandments, the Lord's Prayer, the Ave Maria, the seven sacraments, justification and purgatory. This list of contents suggests that it was still firmly anchored in the Roman Catholic heritage of the English Church, but this is not quite the case. While it does endorse the Roman doctrine of transubstantiation, the inclusion of the article on justification demonstrates some Protestant priorities and the article on purgatory consciously moves away from the Roman teaching. The *Bishops' Book* is therefore best understood as a truly transitional work sitting at the juncture of England's Roman Catholic past and its Protestant future.

A Necessary Doctrine and Erudition for Any Christian Man (commonly known as the King's Book) of 1543

This is a revision of the *Bishops' Book*. As well as discussion on the three core formulations, the sacraments and the Ave Maria, it contains the declaration of faith, articles on free will, justification and good works and a Prayer for Souls Departed. This prayer was a reworking of the *Bishops' Book*'s article on purgatory, and it moves even further away from old Roman doctrine. It boldly admits ignorance regarding the true nature of purgatory and the specific efficacy of prayers for the dead. This is remarkable, given that Henry VIII had unambiguously affirmed the traditional view of purgatory two decades earlier in the opening of his *Defence of the Seven Sacraments*, the work that had earned him title of Defender of the Faith from Leo X.

The A.B.C set forthe by the Kynges maiestie and his cleargye ... of circa. 1545

This is a small publication containing a basic presentation of the Creed, the Ten Commandments and Lord's Prayer as well as some graces to be said at mealtimes and an alphabet.

[Cranmer's Catechism of 1548]

This long catechism set forth by Archbishop Cranmer is actually a translation made by Justus Jonas in 1539 of Andreas Osiander's 1533 Nuremberg sermons, which in turn were expositions of Luther's *Small Catechism* of 1529. It engages with the Creed, Commandments and Paternoster, but then also with the two sacraments and the Keys to the Kingdom, a significant doctrine during the Reformation. The characteristic feature of this catechism is its extensive presentation of justification by faith.

The Catechism (also commonly known as the Church Catechism) of 1549

This short catechism was found in the Confirmation service of the first *Book of Common Prayer* and remained there up until the 1662 edition. It was also reproduced elsewhere, such as in *An, A,B,C, wyth a cathechisme ...* of 1551 and in *King Edward's Primer* of 1553. It contains just the three central formulations of faith in interrogatory style with a bishop filling the master's role. In the 1604 *Book of Common Prayer*, this catechism was revised to include questions on the sacraments.

King Edward's Catechism of 1553

This long catechism was co-published with the *Forty-Two Articles* and is of a different stripe to the preceding long catechisms. While it draws from the *Bishops' Book* and *King's Book*, its theological interests are quite different. It is solidly Protestant, as might be expected for a work produced at the end of Edward VI's reign; more surprising, however, is its strong concern with eschatological matters. Following the questions and answers about the Creed, the master proceeds to drill the student regarding the resurrection and afterlife. Not only is this in contrast to other catechisms of the day, it is also an unusual emphasis for any of the authoritative documents of England's Reformation.

Nowell's Catechisms of 1570 and 1572

Nowell's Long Catechism, or *Full Catechism*, contains discussion of the three formulations and the sacraments, and also gives space to a consideration of the doctrine of Scripture, which by this point had been well solidified as a cornerstone of Protestant belief. Like *King Edward's Catechism*, Alexander Nowell's volume has a notable emphasis on eschatology, although this focus is not as strong as in the earlier work, upon which Nowell certainly did not directly draw. Rather, his volume is marked by a considerable degree of originality throughout. *Nowell's Catechism* was produced in both its full version and an abridged or 'middle' version in 1570. In 1572, a 'small' version also followed, and this last catechism is very similar to the *Church Catechism*.

History

The recognition of the Apostle's Creed, Ten Commandments and Lord's Prayer as the touchstones of the Christian faith dates back to at least Augustine who, in his *Enchiridion*, mapped them onto the Pauline triplet of Christian virtues: faith, hope and love. In 1281, English Archbishop John Peckham required the quarterly teaching of the Creed and Commandments along with the two great commandments, the seven works of mercy, the seven deadly sins, the seven principle virtues and the seven sacraments. By the early modern period, the pattern of providing basic religious instruction around the three formulations was well set.

By producing catechisms built around a standard body of material, the English Reformers were not at all pioneering, but simply continuing a longstanding tradition of the church. What may have been new was the number of catechisms produced and distributed during the Tudor years. It is well known that one of the early uses of the printing press was to greatly increase the supply of Bibles and other religious literature. It is less well known that short catechisms were printed in quantities that far outstripped anything else. Hundreds of thousands of copies were made; one estimate posits that there was a time when there may have been more catechisms in early modern England than people.[1] This shows that the *Church Catechism* was not just an element of an occasional service in the *Book of Common Prayer*; it was the basic summary of Christian teaching that was nearly ubiquitous during the Reformation years.

And the prominence of catechisms was not confined to England. Luther's catechisms are famous, but it is not often recognised that John Calvin's *Institutes of the Christian Religion*, perhaps the single most significant work of Reformation theology, was initially conceived as a catechism. In the original edition of 1536, the first five chapters were respectively on the Ten Commandments, the Creed, the Lord's Prayer, the sacraments and false sacraments. It was only the sixth and final chapter that addressed subject matter other than the standard catechetical formulations and it was only in subsequent revisions of the *Institutes* that Calvin moved away from this catechetical format. Of course, even the first edition of Calvin's *Institutes* was orders of magnitude larger than the English *Church Catechism*. This was because it followed the tradition of presenting the formulations with extended commentary to offer a fuller explanation of the message of the Bible and the fundaments of Christianity.

The large catechisms in England also followed this tradition. Thus the *Bishops' Book*, in its epistle dedicatory, explains that the committee of bishops who compiled the volume had set upon 'the diligent search and perusing of holy scripture, to set forth a plain and sincere doctrine, concerning the whole sum of all those things which appertain unto the profession of a Christian man'.[2] They concluded that –

---

[1] I Green, *Christian's ABC*, p 68.

[2] C Lloyd, *Formularies of Faith Put Forth by Authority During the Reign of Henry VIII* (Oxford: The Clarendon Press, 1825), p 23.

> the whole pith and sum of all those things which be at great length contained in the whole canon of the Bible, and be of necessity required to the attaining of everlasting life, was sufficiently, exactly, and therewith shortly and compendiously comprehended in the twelve articles of the common creed, called the Apostles' Creed, in the Seven Sacraments of the church, in the Ten Commandments, and in the prayer of our Lord, called the Pater noster[3]

The epistle also explains that the inclusion of articles on the doctrines of justification and purgatory in the *Bishops' Book* was not because they were considered equally important as the core triad, but because the compilers did not want to ignore those matters that Henry had given special attention to in the *Ten Articles* of the previous year. The *Bishops' Book* did not bring any fresh thinking to those doctrines, but simply reproduced the relevant parts of the *Ten Articles* unmodified.

Despite the facts that its focus was on the standard catechetical materials, supplemented by articles approved by Henry, the king was not impressed with the *Bishops' Book* and quickly became personally involved in its revision. Henry's notes, and Cranmer's subsequent notes upon those notes, are still extant for those who wish to trace the modifications in detail. The final result of these revisions was the *King's Book* of 1543, which superseded the *Bishops' Book* as it was set forth with great authority and the claim to contain 'perfect and sufficient doctrine'.[4]

Not a great deal is known about the history of *King Edward's Catechism* and *Nowell's Catechism*. The former has sometimes been attributed to Bishop John Ponet, but without much convincing evidence. An early version of the latter, produced by Alexander Nowell, Dean of St Paul's Cathedral, existed in 1563, when it was given formal consideration by the convocation. Both houses assented to it at that time, but it underwent some revisions before being finally promulgated in 1570. Unfortunately, the annotated 1563 copy went missing in the nineteenth century after having been sold in an auction. Resonances with both *King Edward's Catechism* and *Calvin's Catechism* are detectable in Nowell's work, but few lines of direct dependence can be determined. The case is similar for the relationship between *Nowell's Small Catechism* and the

---

[3] Lloyd, *Formularies*, p 24.

[4] Lloyd, *Formularies*, p 217.

Church Catechism. While these are very similar and there has been much speculation on their relationship, there is no firm evidence of common provenance. Any speculations must also account for the fact that all of the short catechisms were similar, and that early modern practices of freely borrowing and recycling of material regularly makes source hunting a great challenge.

Intended Purpose

When Henry included a catechism with the printing of the standard alphabet around 1545, he was not offering his novice readers a popular text on which they might practice their new skill. Rather, he was promulgating the alphabet and encouraging reading in order that people could learn their catechisms. Literacy was not being developed for its own sake but as a means of ensuring a standardised religious education for the masses. This point cannot be stressed too strongly: the purpose of the catechisms was to advance the basic 'Christianisation' of all the people.

In addition to the vast numbers of catechisms printed during the Reformation years, other lines of evidence demonstrate how high a priority Christianisation was for the English Reformers and how centrally catechesis sat in the process. One is the prominence in the parish churches of the huge commandments boards that bore the three formulations; these are still to be found at the front of many Anglican churches today. Another is found in the various sets of Royal Injunctions produced during the Tudor years. The fifth of the Elizabethan Injunctions of 1559 read –

> Item. That every holy day throughout the year, when they [the clergy] have no sermon, they shall immediately after the Gospel openly and plainly recite to their parishioners, in the pulpit, the *Paternoster,* the Creed and the Ten Commandments in English, the intent that the people may learn the same by heart, exhorting all parents and householders to teach their children and servants the same, as they are bound by the law of God and in conscience to do.[5]

[5] G L Bray (ed.), *Documents of the English Reformation* (Cambridge: James Clarke & Co. Ltd, 1994), pp 336–337.

Corresponding items can also be found in the Henrician and Edwardian Injunctions and in the Church canons of 1571 and 1604.

Two important points flow on from this. First, the English Reformers did not want nominalism to abound as the ironic fruit of a Christendom state. They wanted the people to understand and personally affirm the national faith, not just be born into it. This is the reason that they were not only taught the formulations of faith, but were also examined on them at their confirmation. The ninth of the Edwardian Injunctions of 1547 required that all parishioners be able to recite the three formulations before being admitted to communion. Right through until the second half of the seventeenth century, the Confirmation service included the bishop interrogating the catechumen on the formulations as they sought full entry into the life of the Church, and indeed the state. No doubt nominalism persisted for many; the rote learning and recitation of pre-packaged formulations was not an infallible method of Christianising the heart. Nonetheless, the intention of the Church was that all of the people would know and accept the basics of the faith as captured in the Creed, Lord's Prayer and Ten Commandments.

The second point is that in catechising, the English Reformers were seeking the 'Christianisation' of the masses, not their 'Protestantisation', and certainly not their 'Anglicanisation'. The three formulations did not constitute a national Church confession, but were simply the recognised encapsulation of the basic beliefs of the church universal. Significantly, they were not even fundamentally at odds even with Rome, although the exclusion of materials such as the Ave Maria and the inclusion of particular materials regarding the sacraments would make the lines between the Catholics and the Protestants very clear, as would the commentaries of the longer catechisms.

Key References

H Anders, 'The Elizabethan ABC with Catechism', *The Library*, s4–xvi (1), 1935, pp 32–48

This article examines the only known remaining fragment of the Elizabethan ABC, and notes that its admonition of subjects may have been a unique feature.

G L Bray (ed.), *The Institution of a Christian Man* (Cambridge: James Clarke & Co. Ltd, 2018)

This is a composite, critical edition of the *Bishops' Book, King's Book* and *Bishop Bonner's Book*, the equivalent catechism of the Marian period.

G E Corrie (ed.), *A Catechism Written in Latin by Alexander Nowell, Dean of St Paul's* (Cambridge: Cambridge University Press, 1853)

This is a full reprint of *Nowell's Catechism.*

M Davie, *Instruction in the Way of the Lord: A Guide to the Catechism in the Book of Common Prayer* (London: The Latimer Trust, 2014)

This small volume is a good introduction to the *Church Catechism* and includes a helpful concise history of the catechisms, especially as they relate to the rite of Confirmation.

I Green, *The Christian's ABC: Catechisms and Catechizing in England c. 1530–1740* (Oxford: Clarendon Press, 1996)

This is a large volume that presents the results of substantial research into the English catechisms, their production and distribution. It also contains an extensive—if not exhaustive—catalogue of early English catechisms. The *Bishops' Book* is one notable omission from the list.

H Jenkyns (ed.), *The Remains of Thomas Cranmer: Archbishop of Canterbury*, Volume 2 (Oxford: Oxford University Press, 1833)

Jenkyns' volume contains Henry's comments on the *Bishops' Book* and Cranmer's responses. Helpfully, Jenkyns points out that prior to his printing of this material, Cranmer's annotations had been mistakenly, and quite confusingly, considered to have been made on a marked-up copy of the *King's Book*, rather than the *Bishops' Book*. But then adding to the ongoing confusion is the fact that Jenkyns then continues to propagate the error.

J Ketley (ed.), *The Two Liturgies, with other Documents set forth by Authority in the Reign of King Edward VI* (Cambridge: Cambridge University Press, 1844)

Ketley's volume is a standard for the first two *Books of Common Prayer*, but also contains a reprint of *King Edward's Catechism.*

C Lloyd, *Formularies of Faith Put Forth by Authority During the Reign of Henry VIII* (Oxford: The Clarendon Press, 1825)

Lloyd's volume contains the reprints of the *Bishops' Book* and *King's Book* that were standard prior to Bray's more recent publication noted above.

W P McDonald, *Christian Catechetical Texts, Book 1: Medieval and Reformation, 1357–1579* (Lewiston, Queenston, Lampeter: The Edwin Mellen Press, 2011)

This volume contains both an introduction to the catechisms as a type of text as well as the text of many Reformation catechisms individually introduced and discussed.

D G Selwyn, *A Catechism set forth by Thomas Cranmer* (Appleford: Sutton Courtenay Press, 1978)

This is a standard version of Cranmer's Catechism and contains a helpful introduction by Selwyn.

F Watson, *The English Grammar Schools to 1600: their Curriculum and Practice* (Cambridge: Cambridge University Press, 1908), pp 161– 172

These pages give a good introduction to the ABCs.

5. Homilies

Like sermons, homilies were religious lessons to be delivered from the pulpits of parish churches for the instruction of the people. But, although homilies were sometimes called sermons—as was the case for some of those discussed below – it is helpful to make some distinction between a homily and a sermon proper.

During England's Reformation, a sermon was, generally speaking, a religious monologue prepared for a particular occasion and was delivered to its audience by its author. It might have also been based on a particular biblical text, although that was not necessarily so and many sermons were topical. Homilies, on the other hand, were fixed works prepared for widespread and ongoing use by any number of different clerical orators in a range of settings. Most of the preachers of the homilies would have had no personal connection to their authors, and those authors would not be familiar with the particular contexts into which the homilies would be preached. Homilies were usually bound up into collections, and each was therefore received as a part of a package of religious teaching that might be presented over an extended period of time and in many separate church services.

Homilies could focus on the exposition of a single piece of Scripture, deal with more synthetic issues, or even address non-biblical subjects, but one common characteristic of the different collections of Reformation homilies was their heavy use of the Bible throughout. Like the services in the *Books of Common Prayer*, the homilies in these collections were rich with both direct biblical references and non-explicit allusions to the Scriptures. This indicates that their authors had a high regard and close familiarity with the Bible and considerable ability to make extensive use of it in their theological arguments and paradigms. The writings of the church Fathers are also regularly called upon, as they are in other formularies.

Specific Descriptions

Taverner's Postils of 1540

A postil is a brief homily based on a preceding Bible reading.[1] *Taverner's Postils* is a collection of over 160 homilies that were matched to the lectionary readings and liturgical year. The collection is divided into three sub-groupings: the Winter Part, which covered Advent to Holy Week, the Summer Part, which covered Easter to Advent, and the postils for holy days. Within the postils are some with a Catholic focus, celebrating days such as the conception, annunciation and assumption of Mary. For the first two parts, there is a postil given for each Gospel and epistle reading, but for the holy days all of the readings are taken from the Gospels. The only exceptions to this pattern are the postil for the Twelfth Day of Christmas, which is based on Isaiah 60, and the postils on the resurrection and for Rogation Week, which are not based on any single reading. The Athanasian Creed is also printed at the end of the Winter Part.

Each postil has headings indicating for which day it was prepared and which Scripture reading it is based upon. These are followed by a summary or statement of its argument, topic or main point, which is followed in turn by the full body of the homily itself. Many of the postils are around two to three pages long, although some are considerably longer. The postils that make up Taverner's collection are in Table 3.

Table 3. Calendar dates and biblical texts for Taverner's Postils

WINTER PART		
Day	Epistle	Gospel
First Sunday in Advent	Romans 13	Mathew 21
Second Sunday in Advent	Romans 15	Luke 21

[1] The word postil comes from the Latin *post illa,* meaning 'after that'.

Third Sunday in Advent	1 Corinthians 4	Matthew 11
Fourth Sunday in Advent	Philippians 4	John 1
Christmas Day at High Mass	Hebrews 1	John 1
St Steven	Acts 6-7	Matthew 23
St John the Evangelist	Ecclesiastes 15	John 21
Childermas Day	Revelation 14	Matthew 2
Sunday after Christmas Day	Galatians 4	Luke 2
New Year's Day	Titus 2	Luke 2
Twelfth Day	Isaiah 60	Matthew 2
First Sunday after Twelfth Day	-	John 1
Second Sunday after Twelfth Day	Romans 12	Luke 2
Third Sunday after Twelfth Day	Romans 12	John 2
Fourth Sunday after Twelfth Day	Romans 12	Matthew 8
Fifth Sunday after Twelfth Day	Romans 13	Matthew 8
Sixth Sunday after Twelfth Day	Colossians 3	Matthew 8
Septuagesima Sunday	1 Corinthians 13	Matthew 20
Sexagesima Sunday	2 Corinthians 11	Luke 8
Quinquagesima Sunday	1 Corinthians 13	Luke 18
First Sunday in Lent	2 Corinthians 6	Matthew 4
Second Sunday in Lent	1 Thessalonians 4	Matthew 15
Third Sunday in Lent	Ephesians 5	Luke 11

Midlent Sunday	Galatians 4	John 6
Passion Sunday	Hebrews 9	John 8
Palm Sunday	Philippians 2	Matthew 26
Before the Communion	1 Corinthians 11	
Resurrection		
Easter Day	1 Corinthians 5	Mark 16
Monday in Easter Week	Acts 10	Luke 24
Tuesday in Easter Week	Acts 13	Luke 24
Wednesday in Easter Week	Acts 3	John 21
Creed of St Athanasius		
SUMMER PART		
Day	Epistle	Gospel
First Sunday after Easter / Low Sunday	1 John 5	John 20
Second Sunday after Easter	1 Peter 2	John 10
Third Sunday after Easter	1 Peter 2	John 16
Fourth Sunday after Easter	James 1	John 16
Fifth Sunday after Easter	James 1	John 16
Rogation Week		
Ascension Day	Acts 1	Mark 16
Sunday after Ascension Day	1 Peter 4	John 15-16
Whitsunday	Acts 2	John 14

Second Day of Pentecost	Acts 10	John 3
Third Day of Pentecost	Acts 8	John 10
Fourth Day of Pentecost	Acts 2	John 6
Corpus Christi Day	1 Corinthians 11	John 6
Trinity Sunday	Revelation 4	John 3
First Sunday after Trinity	1 John 4	Luke 16
Second Sunday after Trinity	1 John 3	Luke 14
Third Sunday after Trinity	1 Peter 5	Luke 15
Fourth Sunday after Trinity	Romans 8	Luke 6
Fifth Sunday after Trinity	1 Peter 3	Luke 5
Sixth Sunday after Trinity	Romans 6	Matthew 5
Seventh Sunday after Trinity	Romans 6	Mark 8
Eighth Sunday after Trinity	Romans 8	Matthew 7
Ninth Sunday after Trinity	1 Corinthians 10	Luke 16
Tenth Sunday after Trinity	1 Corinthians 12	Luke 19
Eleventh Sunday after Trinity	1 Corinthians 15	Luke 18
Twelfth Sunday after Trinity	2 Corinthians 3	Mark 7
Thirteenth Sunday after Trinity	Galatians 3	Luke 10
Fourteenth Sunday after Trinity	Galatians 5	Luke 17
Fifteenth Sunday after Trinity	Galatians 5-6	Matthew 6
Sixteenth Sunday after Trinity	Ephesians 3	Luke 7

Seventeenth Sunday after Trinity	Ephesians 4	Luke 14
Eighteenth Sunday after Trinity	1 Corinthians 1	Matthew 22
Nineteenth Sunday after Trinity	Ephesians 4	Matthew 9
Twentieth Sunday after Trinity	Ephesians 5	Matthew 22
Twenty-first Sunday after Trinity	Ephesians 6	John 4
Twenty-second Sunday after Trinity	Philippians 1	Matthew 18
Twenty-third Sunday after Trinity	Philippians 3	Matthew 22
Twenty-fourth Sunday after Trinity	Colossians 1	Matthew 9
Twenty-fifth Sunday after Trinity	Jeremiah 23	John 6

HOLY DAYS	
Day	Gospel
St Andrew	Matthew 4
Conception of our Lady	Matthew 1
St Thomas the Apostle	John 20
Candelmas / Purification of our Lady	Luke 2
St Mathias the Aspostle	Matthew 11
Annunciation / Ladies Day in Lent	Luke 1
St George and St Mark the Evangelist	John 15
Philip and Jacob	John 14
St John the Baptist	Luke 1
St Peter and St Paul	Matthew 16

Mary Magdelene	Luke 7
St James the Apostle	Matthew 20
Assumption of our Lady	Luke 10
St Bartholomew	Luke 22
Nativity of our Lady	Matthew 1
St Matthews	Matthew 9
St Michaelmas	Matthew 13
St Luke the Evangelist	Luke 10
St Simon and Jude	John 15
All Hallows Day	Matthew 5
Day of the Wedding	Matthew 19
At Buryings	John 11

The First Book of Homilies of 1547

The First Book of Homilies contains twelve homilies that can be meaningfully divided into two subsets, although no such division is indicated in the collection itself. The first five (or six; different commentators have different views) outline the core Protestant doctrines in their logical sequence. The first homily, on Scripture, opens the collection by establishing the Church's theological authority. The second, on sin, begins to unfold the Protestant *ordo salutis*, which is developed throughout the third, fourth and fifth homilies. (The fourth and fifth homilies form something of a pair, with both addressing the relationship between faith and good works.) The remaining homilies in the *First Book* are mainly concerned with particular expressions of godly living with the exception of the ninth homily, which has a more pastoral focus. The sixth homily is the shortest, at less than three thousand words, and the eleventh is the longest, running to over six thousand words. The homilies that make up the *First Book* are –

1. A Fruitful exhortation to the reading of Holy Scripture
2. Of the misery of all mankind
3. Of the salvation of all mankind
4. Of the true and lively faith
5. Of good works
6. Of Christian love and charity
7. Against swearing and perjury
8. Of the declining from God
9. An exhortation against the fear of death
10. An exhortation to obedience
11. Against whoredom and adultery
12. Against strife and contention

The Second Book of Homilies of 1563

The *Second Book of Homilies* contains twenty new homilies, with one more, An Homily against Disobedience and Wilful Rebellion, added in 1571. The *Second Book* has less of a clear shape than the *First Book*, and most of the homilies in it are directed towards tackling a range of issues concerning church order and morality. Thus, positively, it contains homilies on the sacraments, almsgiving and marriage; negatively, it has homilies against idolatry, gluttony and drunkenness, and idleness. There are some homilies in the collection that are of a different kind and instead map onto the Church's calendar, notably the four that sequentially address Christ's nativity, his passion (two homilies) and his resurrection (lifted directly from *Taverner's Postils*), and the homilies for Whitsunday and Rogation Week, and there is also a triplet on prayer. The homilies in the *Second Book* vary greatly in length with the longest, on idolatry, running to nearly thirty-seven thousand words while shortest, on the maintenance and cleaning of the church, is just over two thousand. Other long homilies in the collection are the seventeenth on Rogation week and twentieth on repentance, around ten thousand words apiece, and the final sermon on rebellion at over twenty thousand words. The homilies that make up the *Second Book* are –

1. Of the right use of the Church
2. Against peril of Idolatry
3. For repairing and keeping clean the Church
4. Of good works. And first of Fasting
5. Against gluttony and drunkenness
6. Against excesse of apparel
7. An Homilie of Prayer
8. Of the place and time of Prayer
9. Of Common Prayer and Sacraments
10. An information of them which take offence at certain places of holy Scripture
11. Of alms deeds
12. Of the Nativity
13. Of the Passion for Good Friday
14. Of the Resurrection for Easter day
15. Of the worthy receiving of the Sacrament
16. An Homilie concerning the coming down of the holy Ghost, for Whitsunday
17. An Homilie for Rogation week
18. Of the state of Matrimony
19. Against Idleness
20. Of Repentance and true Reconciliation unto God
21. An Homily against disobedience and wilful rebellion [added in 1571]

Since 1623 the homilies have usually been collected together in a single volume. Individual homilies are now divided into two or three smaller parts (with just An Homily against Disobedience and Willful Rebellion divided into six), thus effectively creating 72 mini-homilies out of the official 33.

History

In the medieval period, it was not uncommon for parish preachers to rely heavily on collections of prepared homilies as the sources of their weekly messages. There were two main reasons for this. The first was simply that clergy were neither trained nor viewed as preachers (in the modern concept of that office). Their work was not so much about reflecting on the Scriptures or the faith and then delivering their thoughts to the people; it was more ceremonial and sacramental, concerned with the rituals of religious life for their communities. As such, few of the parish clergy were expected to be gifted in preaching. It was only during the post-Reformation years that preaching came to be seen as their emblematic and core duty. Given this, it was quite normal for preaching to be no more than the reading out of a homily from an established collection. Clergy would not have been considered substandard or derelict in their duty for doing this; it was standard practice.

The second reason that clergy mainly read out prepared homilies relates to the subject matter of most late medieval preaching. Because the cult of the saints so dominated the religious life of the time, there were relatively few days in the year that did not commemorate a saint or festival. As a result, preaching tended to focus on the lives of the saints, and much preaching was no more than reading out stories from the popular hagiographies such as William Caxton's *Legenda Aurea* and John Mirk's *Liber Festivalis*.

Bible-based preaching was, of course, one of the hallmarks and lasting fruits of the Reformation, and in the sixteenth century the new homiliaries were produced to replace the hagiographies. In 1540, Richard Taverner (the reviser of *Matthew's Bible*) produced a substantial collection of homilies known as the *Postils*, almost all of which were reflections on single chapters of the New Testament. It is not clear how much these postils reflect the views of Taverner himself; in his preface, he does not claim to have authored the whole collection but only to have written some and compiled others. A strong contender for one of Taverner's main sources is a collection of postils, now lost, that the Lutheran Erasmus Sarcerius had dedicated to Henry VIII. Sarcerius was well known to Taverner, who had translated his theological work

Common Places. It has also been suggested that some of the postils draw from the *Paraphrases* of Erasmus of Rotterdam (discussed further in chapter 8).

Taverner's *Postils* marked a significant departure from the Roman homiliaries, but it was short lived. During the convocation of 1541–1543, the English bishops laid out a plan to prepare an official collection of homilies for the Church. Stephen Gardiner, the conservative bishop of Winchester, stated that the purpose of the new homilies was 'for stay of such errors as were then by ignorant preachers sparkled among the people', although his views of the Church's errors at this stage may not have been the same as those of his more reform-minded colleagues.[2] By 1547, the collection, now known as the *First Book of Homilies*, was complete, and the Royal Injunctions of the same year proclaimed –

> Also because through lack of preachers in many places of the King's realms and dominions the people continue in ignorance and blindness, all parsons, vicars and curates shall read in their churches every Sunday one of the homilies which are and shall be set forth for the same purpose, by the King's authority in such sort as they shall be appointed to do, in the preface of the same.[3]

Another of Edward VI's Injunctions stated –

> Item, that they [the clergy] shall admit no man to preach within any of their cures, but such as shall appear unto them to be sufficiently licensed thereunto by the King's Majesty, the Lord Protector's grace, the Archbishop of Canterbury, the Archbishop of York in his province or the bishop of the diocese. And such as shall be so licensed they shall gladly receive to declare the Word of God, without any resistance or contradiction.[4]

Given that few such preaching licenses were issued, these two Injunctions meant that teaching from the majority of England's pulpits was limited to the homilies of the *First Book*, a radical change from

---

[2] Quoted in J Griffiths (ed.), *The Two Books of Homilies Appointed to be Read in Churches* (Oxford: Oxford University Press, 1859), p vii.

[3] Bray, *Documents*, p 256.

[4] Bray, *Documents*, p 251.

medieval practice. Indeed, even Taverner in his preface to the *Postils* commends his collection to priests and curates for the feeding of the flock, but also approves of them using their own compositions if they felt they could do better. When Elizabeth I came to power, her 1559 Injunctions re-established the Edwardian position.

Although there were only twelve homilies in the *First Book*, in 1549 they were sub-divided into 32 parts, meaning that instead of the whole collection being heard about four times per year (assuming the homilies were only rehearsed on Sundays) it would be heard less than twice. While this might have given the Church a more varied diet, Martin Bucer, then resident in Cambridge, objected to the homilies being 'cut short' in this way.[5]

In both the first of the Edwardian Injunctions and its Elizabethan equivalent, there is an expectation that more homilies 'shall be set forth'. This echoes the postscript to the *First Book*, which reads –

> Hereafter shall follow sermons of fasting, praing, alms deeds, of the nativity, passion, resurrection and ascension of our Saviour Christ; of the due receiving of his blessed body and blood under the form of bread and wine; against idleness, against gluttony and drunkenness, against covetousness, against envy, ire, and malice; with many other matters as well as fruitful as necessary to the edifying of Christian people and the increase of godly living. Amen.[6]

This intention was fulfilled in the *Second Book of Homilies* of 1563, which was more fully entitled *The Second Part of Homilies, of Such Matters as were Promised and Entitled in the Former Part of Homilies.* Thus, the division of the homilies into two books should not be taken to indicate that they were distinct collections. Rather, they were always intended to be two parts of a unified whole, separated by time only because of the return to Catholicism for the years of Mary's rule. When the *Second Book of Homilies* was promulgated, the *First Book* was also reissued with some very minor editorial changes. The full collection was completed in 1571 with the addition of An Homily against Disobedience

---

[5] E C Whitaker, *Martin Bucer and The Book of Common Prayer* (Great Wakering: Mayhew-McCrimmon, 1974), p 46.

[6] G L Bray (ed.), *The Book of Homilies, A Critical Edition* (Cambridge: James Clarke & Co, 2015), p 119.

and Wilful Rebellion, written in the aftermath of the Northern Rebellion of 1569 and Pope Pius' bull, *Regnans in Excelcis*, which had seen Elizabeth excommunicated from the Catholic Church and her Catholic subjects released from her rule.

Intended Purpose

As made clear in the Injunctions, the purpose of the two *Books of Homilies* was to provide sound teaching in churches and in doing so, to compensate for the lack of able preachers in England. By issuing a standardised set of teachings for the pulpits of parish churches, any cleric who could read could deliver newly approved doctrine to the people, and no variant theology would be preached to undiscerning congregants. This was a prime strategic move in the progress of the English Reformation, and indeed one of the first public moves, predating the reform of the Church's services. But having a set of homilies that were doctrinal rather than expositional meant that the people would not be taught the meaning of the many different texts of Scripture and neither would Scripture be used to continually shape and inform their theology. There was no connection between text and sermon. Bible readings were determined by Cranmer's revised Kalendars, which employed the *lectio continua* principle, but the sermon that followed would have nothing to do with the passage read. It is worth making the point explicit: despite the Protestant priorities, and even the subject of the first homily, the Reformers' intention for the homilies was not to teach people the Bible itself, but instead to teach them a systematic doctrinal framework. To be sure, this framework was drawn from the Bible, but it was a synthetic construct that did not address the fullness of subjects found in the Scriptures.

This limitation was apparent to Elizabeth's second Archbishop of Canterbury, Edmund Grindal. When the Queen wanted to close down the 'prophesyings' that had begun under the Puritan influence, Grindal courageously opposed her. These prophesyings were essentially practical, interactive workshops for coaching young preachers. Grindal saw these gatherings as an important means for raising up a new generation of preachers and moving on from the two *Books of Homilies*, which he felt could only be accepted as a stop-gap measure. Elizabeth, however, saw things differently. She felt that there were too many risks in allowing more clergy to prepare their own sermons from the Bible and so required the two *Books of Homilies* to remain as the fixed standard of preached doctrine.

Key References

G L Bray (ed.), *The Book of Homilies, A Critical Edition* (Cambridge: James Clarke & Co, 2015)

This is a recent critical edition of the *Books of Homilies*. It includes a valuable introduction and all of Bishop Bonner's Marian homilies in addition to the Edwardian and Elizabethan homilies.

G L Bray, *A Fruitful Exhortation: A Guide to the Homilies* (London: The Latimer Trust, 2014)

This is a lighter introduction to the *First Book* and *Second Book of Homilies* and each of the individual homilies they contain, and it also supplies extracts of key passages from all of the homilies.

E Cardwell (ed.), *Postils on the Epistles and Gospels Compiled and Published by Richard Taverner in the year 1540* (Oxford: Oxford University Press, 1841)

This volume contains all of Taverner's postils.

P Collinson, *Archbishop Grindal 1519–1583: The Struggle for a Reformed Church* (London: Jonathan Cape, 1979)

The story of Grindal's conflict with Elizabeth over the prophesyings can be found on pages 233–252 of this volume.

L Gatiss, *Edmund Grindal: The Preacher's Archbishop* (London: The Latimer Trust, 2013)

Another helpful volume that discusses the conflict between Grindal and Elizabeth.

J Griffiths (ed.), *The Two Books of Homilies Appointed to be Read in Churches* (Oxford: Oxford University Press, 1859)

As well as providing the text of all the homilies, Griffiths offers a helpful overview of their development in his introduction. This was the standard critical edition before Bray's more recent volume noted above.

I Morgan, *The Godly Preachers of the Elizabethan Church* (London: The Epworth Press, 1965)

Pages 68–74 of Morgan's book give a good introduction to the prophesyings of Grindal's day and their historical setting.

A Null, 'Official Tudor Homilies' in P McCullough, H Adlington and E Rhatigan (eds), *The Oxford Handbook of the Early Modern Sermon* (Oxford: Oxford University Press, 2011)

Like all of Ashley Null's work, this is a beautifully written chapter that is clear, detailed and comprehensive in scope. It is perhaps the best available short introduction to the two *Books of Homilies*.

S Wabuda, *Preaching During the English Reformation* (Cambridge: Cambridge University Press, 2002)

This volume considers preaching during England's Reformation and includes helpful analysis of the different types of preaching and their purposes.

6. The Ordinal

The *Ordinal* is the name given to the text of the three liturgical services that are together formally entitled *The Form and Manner of Making, Ordaining and Consecrating of Bishops, Priests and Deacons According to the Order of the Church of England.* It is now almost always included at the end of the *Book of Common Prayer,* although, like Confirmation, these services cannot be conducted by lower clergy. Both *The Form and Manner of Making of Deacons* and *The Form and Manner of Ordering of Priests* must be led by the local bishop, with an archdeacon, or their substitute, in attendance. *The Form of Ordaining or Consecrating of an Archbishop or Bishop* must be led by the archbishop or an alternatively appointed bishop, with two other bishops also participating. When they are conducted, each of the three services begins with Morning Prayer and includes sharing in Communion after the aspirants have been admitted to the orders.

Each service also includes a formal presentation of the aspirants, many prayers, set Bible readings, an examination, an oath of due obedience (omitted in the case where it is an archbishop being consecrated), the laying on of hands and a charge of office. Bishops-elect are also vested after their examination. The readings for the ordination of deacons are either 1 Timothy 3:8–13 or Acts 6:2–7 and Luke 12:35–38. For the ordination of priests they are Ephesians 4:7–13 and either Matthew 9:36–38 or John 10:1–16. For the consecration to the episcopate they are 1 Timothy 3:1–7 or Acts 20:17–35 and one of John 21:15–17, John 20:19–23 or Matthew 28:18–20.

In the presentations and examinations, the *Ordinal* upholds high standards of morality and doctrine for the clergy. It also conceives of a clergyman as holding an office with a particular set of authorities and duties attached. So, the deacons are to publicly read the Gospel, to preach if they are licensed to do so, to assist in serving communion, to catechise the church's youth, to care for the poor and, in the absence of the priest, to baptise. Priests are to pastor, teach and warn, to seek the lost and apostate, to drive out false doctrine and to minister the sacraments. Finally, bishops are to govern, teach, drive out false doctrine, care for the flock and ordain.

History

The *Ordinal* found in the 1662 *Book of Common Prayer* does not differ greatly from the first *Ordinal* of 1549, which was included in the *First Book of Common Prayer* from 1550. The services in the final form have fewer collects than were originally present and have also had the oath of the king's supremacy removed. The service for the ordination of priests has been slightly rearranged, with the hymn *Veni Creator Spiritus* and its alternative moved from the opening of the service to their present position before the laying on of hands. But the most significant change has been to the Bible readings used in the ordination of priests and consecration of bishops. In 1549, the primary reading for the former service was to be either Acts 20:17–35 or all of 1 Timothy 3:1–16 and the secondary reading was to be one of Matthew 9:36–38, John 10:1–16 or John 20:19–23. The primary reading for the consecration of bishops was to be 1 Timothy 3:1–7 and the secondary either John 21:15–17 or John 10:1–16. For clarity, this is presented alongside the readings for 1662 as listed in Table 4.[1]

Table 4. Scripture readings in the *Ordinal*

	1549		1662	
	one of	**plus one of**	**one of**	**plus one of**
Deacons	1 Timothy 3:8–16 Acts 6:2–7		1 Timothy 3:8–13 Acts 6:2–7	Luke 12:35–38
Priests	Acts 20:17–35 1 Timothy 3:1–16	Matthew 9:36–38 John 10:1–16 John 20:19–23	Ephesians 4:7–13	Matthew 9:36–38 John 10:1–16

[1] From T Patrick, 'The Pastoral Offices in the Pastoral Epistles and the Church of England's First Ordinal' in B S Rosner et al. (eds), *Paul as Pastor* (London: Bloomsbury T&T Clark, 2018).

Bishops	1 Timothy 3:1–7	John 21:15–17 John 10:1–16	1 Timothy 3:1–7 Acts 20:17–35	John 21:15–17 John 20:19–23 Matthew 28:18–20

Two things are apparent when considering these changes. The first is that in the 1662 text, there are no readings common to the two services—nor to those used in the ordination of deacons. This is unlike the 1549 version, which offered the 1 Timothy 3 and John 10 passages both for ordaining priests and for consecrating bishops. It also used the same 1 Timothy 3 text for ordaining both priests and deacons. The development to tie each office to different Bible readings suggests that there was some dissatisfaction with the texts originally doing double duty, most likely because that did not allow for a clear distinction between the orders on the basis of what Scripture taught.

The second thing to note is that some of the Bible readings moved from one service to another. While in 1549, John 20 and Acts 20 were considered most appropriate for the ordination of priests, by 1662 they were thought better for the consecration of bishops. Both of these observations indicate that when the famous 'threefold order' of ministry was established in 1549, its biblical basis had not been solidly established.

Deacons, priests and bishops were not new orders of the Reformation but were carried over from the structures of the medieval Roman Catholic Church. For Rome, however, they were not the only clerical orders. Under the ultimate head of its successive popes, the Roman Church's clergy were of two types, the secular and the regular.

The secular clergy were engaged in the work of running the parish churches with their liturgical services and pastoral functions and could be divided into the minor and major orders. In the minor orders were porters, lectors, exorcists and acolytes. In the major orders were subdeacons, deacons, priests, bishops and archbishops, and cardinals. Together, the major orders formed a potential vocational pathway, with all of the priests being drawn from the deacons, all of the bishops being drawn from the priests and so on.

The regular clergy were so named because they lived according to various regulatory vows, or rules. They were of two types, the monastics and the mendicants. Unlike the secular clergy, monastics could be male or female with the males being monks overseen by an abbot and the females being nuns overseen by an abbess. Like the secular clergy, there was a pathway through the monastic orders that started with aspirants, called novices, who could then be admitted as monks or nuns, who in turn might become abbots or abbesses. While the monastics tended to be cloistered and to serve by prayer, scholarship and care for the poor, the mendicants, or friars, were engaged in public and itinerant preaching ministries, even though in later times they could be attached to priories or friaries. In late medieval England there were several orders of mendicants including the blackfriars, grey friars and Austin friars.

As well as working from this history as they established the threefold order, the English Reformers also gave particular ear to Martin Bucer, Regius Professor of Divinity at Cambridge from 1549 to his death in 1551. In his *De ordinatione legitima,* Bucer affirmed two possible categorisations of clergy. First, a two-fold division into overseers (or presbyters) and deacons, and second, the notion of a single ministry office of the presbyter, although with three sub-orders of bishops, presbyters (confusingly) and deacons. This second conception is very close to what is seen in the *Ordinal,* and may throw a little extra light upon it. If the English Reformers were following Bucer's second scheme, it may be that in their understanding, bishops, priests and deacons differed only in degree, not kind.

Intended Purpose

The preface to the *Ordinal* states –

> IT is evident unto all men diligently reading holy Scripture and ancient Authors, that from the Apostles' time there have been these Orders of Ministers in Christ's Church; Bishops, Priests, and Deacons. ... And therefore, to the intent that these Orders may be continued, and reverently used and esteemed, in the Church of England; No man shall be accounted or taken to be a lawful Bishop, Priest, or Deacon in the Church of England, or suffered to execute any of the said functions, except he be called, tried, examined, and admitted thereunto, according to the Form hereafter following, or hath had formerly Episcopal Consecration or Ordination.

In formalising the threefold order, the makers of the *Ordinal* were seeking to restore and uphold New Testament and early church practice. However, the original assignment of Scripture readings to the different services and their subsequent redistribution shows that in 1549, there was no common reading of Scripture that underpinned the idea of three separate orders. Indeed, it remains difficult to argue that presbyters and overseers ('priests' and bishops) are distinguished from each other in the New Testament. It may have been that the English Church was at this point less influenced by 'holy Scripture' and more by 'ancient Authors' such as Ignatius of Antioch, who made the first strong case for monepiscopacy in the early second century.

One important goal of the *Ordinal* was to sever any residual links between England and Rome. In 1534, legislation had passed through the Reformation Parliament that made Henry VIII Supreme Head of the Church in his realms and disallowed any appeals to Rome. The *Ordinal* made it plain that there were no higher offices in the English Church than the bishops and archbishops and that these had authority to legitimately ordain new clergy according to its reformed rites. With both in place, independent England could have an ongoing supply of Protestant clergy who would have no connection or recourse whatsoever to the Roman Catholic Church. Further to this, in heavily paring back the old and more extensive Catholic structures, the English Reformers both declericalised the minor orders of the secular clergy and also completely did away with the regular clergy. The latter was, of course, fully consistent with Henry's dissolution of the monasteries. Like much of the English Reformation, there was a considerable measure of politics commingled with the theological developments.

Key References

F E Brightman, *The English Rite: Being a Synopsis of the Sources and Revisions of the Book of Common Prayer*, Volume 2 (London: Rivingtons, 1921)

Brightman's volumes are indispensable for anyone studying the *Book of Common Prayer* as they present the sources along with the full texts of the 1549, 1552 and 1661/2 editions in parallel columns, allowing developments to be easily traced. Given that the *Ordinal* has been bound with the *BCP* since 1550, it is included in the second volume.

P F Bradshaw, *The Anglican Ordinal: Its History and Development from the Reformation to the Present Day* (London: S.P.C.K., 1971)

This is one of the most complete standard studies of the *Ordinal*.

P F Bradshaw, 'Ordinals' in S Sykes, J Booty, and J Knight (eds), *The Study of Anglicanism*, Revised Edition (London & Minneapolis: SPCK & Fortress Press, 1998)

This is Bradshaw's chapter-length treatment of the *Ordinals*.

G Carey, 'The Origins of the Threefold Christian Ministry', *Churchman*, 96 (1), 1982, 36–43

Written before he became Archbishop of Canterbury, Carey's article offers a helpful analysis of the development of the threefold ministry during the time of the church Fathers.

J N Collins, *Diakonia: Re-interpreting the Ancient Sources* (Oxford: University Press, 1990)

This volume offers perhaps the fullest single exploration of the diaconate. However, it does not spend a great deal of time exploring the office of deacon. That can be found, in Collins' follow up volume (see below).

J N Collins, *Diakonia Studies: Critical Issues in Ministry* (Oxford: University Press, 2014), chapter 7

In line with his thesis that deacons are very much ministers of the word, this chapter gives a remarkable evaluation of the opening verses of Acts 6. Collins makes a strong case that the seven were, in fact, set aside as Greek-speaking counterparts to the Apostles. The case is not incontestable, but it certainly bears consideration.

T Patrick, 'The Pastoral Offices in the Pastoral Epistles and the Church of England's First Ordinal' in B S Rosner, A S Malone and T J Burke (eds), *Paul as Pastor*, (London: Bloomsbury T&T Clark, 2018)

This chapter is a discussion of the offices of church leadership in 1 and 2 Timothy and Titus, with a comparison to the offices prescribed in the *Ordinal*.

A Roberts and J Donaldson (eds), *The Ante-Nicene Fathers, Volume 1: The Apostolic Fathers with Justin Martyr and Irenæus* (Grand Rapids: Wm. B. Eerdmans Publishing Company, 1981)

This volume contains the letters of Ignatius in which he presents his views on the monepiscopate.

7. Primers

Primers were books containing materials to be used in private devotions. While their contents were variable, they tended to include several psalms, often from a recognised subset such as the seven penitential psalms, a dirge, which was a form of prayers to be said either for or in remembrance of the dead, and a set of canonical hours. 'Canonical hours' was the term given to the different times in the day when certain prayers were to be said and, by extension, to the forms of those prayers themselves. So, for example, Mattins was the 'hour' of the dawn and the name given to the prayers that would be said at that time. Prime was the first 'hour' of the day and the name given to prayers said at that time, and so on. There were different sets of hours with different devotional emphases extant in late medieval England and not all primers contained the same ones. Some primers would have the Hours of the Blessed Virgin Mary while others would have the Hours of the Cross and yet others, the Hours of the Holy Spirit. So central were these hours that primers are often alternatively referred to as 'Books of Hours'. In addition to the psalms, dirge and hours, primers also commonly included the central elements of the catechisms, the Apostles' Creed, Ten Commandments and Lord's Prayer, as well as a variety of other prayers.

Primers were usually printed as quarto or octavo volumes rather than large folios, which were not as well suited to personal prayer. Some primers belonging to wealthier people were ornate in their decoration and binding, indicating something of the value that was placed upon them; indeed, personal primers could be held as one of the most deeply treasured of a person's possessions. Many of the most beautifully illuminated manuscripts of the late medieval period are primers. However, the standardised primers of the Tudors lost much of their elaborate decoration because they were reproduced en masse by printing presses and not individually by scribes and fine artists.

Specific Descriptions

King Henry's Primer of 1545

This was the first primer to receive royal privilege, and its title page states that there is 'none other to be used throughout all his [Henry VIII's] dominions'.[1] This command is strongly reinforced in the Injunction printed within the primer, making it clear that the king would not allow even private devotions to be in any form other than that which he had approved. Somewhat surprisingly given its date, this primer is quite unreformed, containing not only the Ave Maria, but also prayers for the dead, and a strikingly dualistic closing prayer that regards the human body as 'the very dark and filthy prison of the soul'. The contents of *King Henry's Primer* are –

- Liturgical calendar
- Lord's Prayer
- Ave Maria
- Apostles' Creed
- Ten Commandments
- Mealtime graces
- Mattins
- Evensong
- Compline
- Psalms
- Litany
- Dirge and commendations
- Christ's passion from John's Gospel
- Prayers for other occasions

King Edward's Primer of 1553

This primer, alternatively known as the *Seres' Primer* after its printer William Seres, is shorter than its predecessor and lacks the litany, dirge, passion narrative and psalms that dominated earlier primers. A large portion of the material in this primer was drawn from the *Book of Common Prayer*, reflecting the latter's growing dominance and perhaps its usefulness and popularity for private, as well as public, devotions. The contents of *King Edward's Primer* are –

- Liturgical calendar
- Church catechism
- Graces
- Instructions for prayer

[1] E Burton, *Three Primers put forth in the Reign of Henry VIII* (Oxford: Oxford University Press, 1834), p 437.

- Morning Prayer (for each day of the week)
- Evening Prayer (for each day of the week)
- Collects
- Sundry Godly Prayers for Diverse Purposes [including for people in different stations and circumstances]

Queen Elizabeth's Primer of 1559

Queen Elizabeth's Primer is essentially a reissue of *King Henry's Primer*, although with some changes. The contents are rearranged, a short order of Morning Prayer has been added and some of the Roman Catholic contents stripped out, including the Ave Maria, the Litany's call for intercessions by the Holy virgin Mari, the angels, spirits and departed saints, and some of the dirge's prayers for the dead. Oddly, however, other non-Protestant elements remain in place such as further prayers for the dead in the dirge and the dualistic closing prayer. The overall result is a primer that is quite confusing in its theological position.

The Orarium seu Libellus Precationem per Regiam of 1560

The *Orarium* is a Latin translation of the *Queen Elizabeth's Primer*, although it varies from the English version in that it opens with the Church Catechism and is without the dirge and commendations. (Henry had also approved a Latin translation of his 1545 primer to be used alongside the English.)

Preces Privatae in Studiosorum Gratiam Collectae of 1564

The *Preces Privatae* is another Latin primer with similar contents to the *Orarium*—a calendar, catechism, morning and evening prayer, litany, graces and various prayers—but including sets of psalms and prayers based on the birth, passion, resurrection and ascension of Christ, as well as others based on the mission of the Spirit and the Trinity.

Book of Christian Prayers of 1578

This collection is quite unlike those that preceded it, being simply a large collection of short prayers for various circumstances, ranging from one paragraph to couple of pages each. These are the types of prayers found appended to the end of some of the other primers now forming the entire substance of a devotional volume. The only standard liturgical resource included is the Litany and Suffrages, which come towards the end of the volume. Aside from its unusual contents, this volume is most distinct for its ornamentation, with decorative and illustrative woodcuts throughout.

History

The primers seem to have evolved from at least two sources: the first, the collections of hours that were said by the regular clergy in the monasteries and convents, and the second, the independently bound and circulated early English Psalters. By the late medieval period, primers often included the standard catechetical formulations along with other materials suitable for devotions in a private home. Boosting their appeal was the fact that they contained more English-language Scripture than any other pre-Reformation volumes, making them the most accessible Bible-rich religious works available to the common people. English primers were often even brought into the church services by lay people who would read from them in the pews, sometimes gathering in small groups to do so. This was one way of turning regular attendance at a Latin ritual into a more meaningful spiritual experience. But given that the various primers of the late medieval period were neither standardised nor authorised by the Church, they were of no use for enforcing uniformity or maintaining doctrinal purity.

In the sixteenth century, this began to change as some important early Protestant primers were produced by George Joye, William Marshall and Thomas Godfray. Joye's *Hortulus Animae* of 1529 excluded the litany and dirge—which had traditionally been the liturgical homes of much Roman doctrine—and was criticised by Thomas More for doing so. Marshall's first primer of 1534 similarly kept these out and also replaced the Hours of the Blessed Virgin Mary with less distinctly Roman canonical hours. In his second edition of 1535, entitled *A Goodly Primer in English*, Marshall reinstated the litany and dirge, but this was clearly done reluctantly and under some pressure. His objections to these parts of the primer were made overt in his strongly negative introductions to them. Thus, the long preface to the dirge included the following –

> Amongst all other works of darkness and deep ignorance, wherein we have blindly wandered, following a sort of blind guides, many days and years, I accompt not this one of the least, that we have run and sung, mumbled and murmured, and piteousy puled forth, a certain sorts of psalms, hereafter ensuing, with responses, versicles, and lessons to the same,

> for the souls of our Christian brethren and sisters that be departed out of this world[2]

This was pointed at the doctrine of purgatory, a pillar of Roman theology that also served as a powerful instrument of control for the Catholic Church. To underscore the error of finding evidence for purgatory in any of the text used in the dirge, Marshall concluded his preface by saying that 'there is nothing in the Dirige taken out of Scripture, that maketh any more mention of the souls departed than doth the tale of Robin Hood'.[3] *Godfray's Primer* of around 1534–35 was a reworked version of Marshall's first primer, although it excluded his negative prefaces and included the accounts of Christ's resurrection and ascension, whereas Marshall had only given the passion.

After these early primers that were more or less Protestant, Bishop Hilsey produced his *Manual of Prayers* in 1539. This had some official support from Cromwell and, more reservedly, from Cranmer. The *Manual* was less Protestant in flavour, although in parts it worked to soften some Roman Catholic teaching. Prayers to the saints were cut back, not because they were always considered to be wrong, but to 'avoid prolixity, which often time decayeth devotion'.[4] Similarly, the 'Fifteen Oes of St Bridget', a part of the liturgy often recited on the understanding that it secured the release of souls from purgatory, were kept, but recast as 'a goodly and godly meditation of Christ's passion'.[5] Despite this diplomatic approach in parts of Hilsey's *Manual*, other parts were more directly aggressive towards the doctrines of the Reformation. Prayers for the dead were retained and the Swiss Reformer Ulrich Zwingli was openly attacked in the promotion of the doctrine of the Real Presence of Christ in the Eucharist.

Against this backdrop, where the primers had a high appeal among the laypeople and versions with different theological flavours were vying for popular acceptance, Henry VIII issued his primer in 1545 to the exclusion of all others. Henry's primer was not novel in its shape and content, as it closely followed in the footsteps of Marshall's and Hilsey's. Its significance, however, was that it marked the end of the period where

---

[2] Burton, *Three Primers*, p 232.
[3] Burton, *Three Primers*, p 234.
[4] Burton, *Three Primers*, p 323.
[5] Burton, *Three Primers*, p 371.

theological diversity would be accepted as a normal part of private devotions. In 1547, Edward VI reissued this primer with few material changes, but by the time his own primer of 1553 was promulgated the overall significance of the primers had begun to wane. This seems to have been a direct effect of the advent of the English Bibles and *Books of Common Prayer*, which had given broad public access to the Scriptures and to materials designed for devotion in the common tongue. With these books in mass circulation, the primers lost a significant part of their niche and purpose. By the seventeenth century the primers, which had often included the contents of the catechisms, had become fully conflated with them. Hence in 1670, during the reign of Charles II, an official volume was produced, entitled, *The Primer or Catechism set forth agreeable to the Book of Common Prayer authorised by the King's majesty to be used throughout all his realms and dominions.*

Intended Purpose

At a basic level, the official primers were intended to furnish the common people with a good breadth of useful materials for their private devotions. The Church did not see its ministry as restricted to Sunday, but expected that all baptised believers would have active personal spiritual lives, which it therefore had some responsibility to both encourage and resource. The fact that the materials were nationally standardised can be viewed as both positive and negative. Positively, uniformity of devotional resources reflected the Church's commitment to promulgating a consistent Protestant theology, something that is understandable and commendable given the context where many Roman, and other non-orthodox, beliefs were practiced. To allow people to privately hold a false doctrine was tantamount to a neglect of pastoral care that would let them wander off the path of true religion. The Church was not going to be satisfied with establishing common forms and substance for public worship while leaving private devotions variable and unreformed. More negatively, the authorisation of just a single primer at any given time was a way of exercising control. Personal preferences and independent reflection on theology was restricted by not allowing the people to practice, or even to consider, differently conceived religion. This, of course, is the same tension already seen in the production of English language Bibles. On the one hand is the desire to clearly lead the people into the truth as understood by the leaders of the Church, but on the other is the conviction that the people should not have the freedom to explore or experience the faith in ways of their own choosing.

Key References

E Burton, *Three Primers put forth in the Reign of Henry VIII* (Oxford: Oxford University Press, 1834)

This volume supplies Marshall's *Goodly Primer*, Hilsey's *Manual of Prayers* and *King Henry's Primer*, along with a useful introduction to all three.

C C Butterworth, *The English Primers (1529–1545)* (Philadelphia: University of Philadelphia Press, 1953)

Butterworth opens this volume by commenting on how little has been written on the English primers and then proceeds throughout to fill the gap admirably. This work traces the history of the production of the primers through Henry's reign and gives consideration of their content before glancing forward to those that followed.

W K Clay, *Private Prayers, put forth by Authority during the Reign of Queen Elizabeth* (Cambridge: Cambridge University Press, 1851)

This Parker Society volume gives the official primers produced during Elizabeth's reign: the *Primer of 1559*, the *Orarium*, the *Preces Privatae* and the *Book of Christian Prayers*. It is also furnished with a useful introduction to them.

J Harthan, *Books of Hours and their Owners* (London: Thames and Hudson, 1977)

Harthan's work is as much an art book as a history book and contains many full-page, full-colour, glossy reproductions of pages from various books of hours. Most of the books showcased pre-date the Reformation and it is only the last brief chapter that considers printed books of hours (where there is a black and white reproduction of a page from the *Book of Christian Prayers*). Nonetheless, this work gives a feel for the aesthetic of the materials that gave rise to the official English primers.

J Ketley, (ed.), *The Two Liturgies, with other Documents set forth by Authority in the Reign of King Edward VI* (Cambridge: Cambridge University Press, 1844)

Ketley's volume is a standard for the first two *Books of Common Prayer* but also contains a reprint of *King Edward's Primer.*

H White, *The Tudor Books of Private Devotion* (Madison: The University of Wisconsin Press, 1951)

Somewhat similar in focus to Butterworth's volume, this work is a helpful and thorough introduction to the primers. Helen White worked for many years on the primers and has other publications on them for those who are interested.

8. Erasmus' Paraphrases and Foxe's 'Book of Martyrs'

The two works considered in this chapter are not connected. Nonetheless, they are treated together here because, unlike the other formularies, neither was produced by the Church establishment. Instead, they received sanction only after they were in circulation, being adopted by, rather than prepared for, the Church. Additionally, there was no requirement that these works should be read or heard by anyone, but only that they be owned by some and made available for those who might want to read them.

ERASMUS' *PARAPHRASES*

Originally penned in Latin, the *Paraphrases* of Desiderius Erasmus of Rotterdam are a running expositional commentary on the text of the New Testament. Similar to many modern day commentaries, the *Paraphrases* present pericopes of the text followed by extended explanations of their meaning, and in this manner they work sequentially through each of the New Testament books from start to finish. Unlike many modern commentaries, the *Paraphrases* do not just offer technical exegesis but include hortatory expositions of the passages and their key ideas, reading more like transcribed sermons than scholarly digests as they address the will as much as the mind.

The English translations were prepared in two large tomes, each one of similar size and appearance to the great lectern Bibles. The first covered the Gospels and Acts, and the second covered the remainder of the New Testament.

History

Erasmus, who lived and worked at the dawn of the Reformation, is rightly famous for two reasons. The first is that he produced several important texts that have had wide impact, both in their day and ongoingly. Among these were a new Greek manuscript of the New Testament, which would be taken as the starting point for many of the Protestant translations of the sixteenth century, and which established the practice of defining and working from a *textus receptus* in biblical studies. Another of his important volumes was *Enchiridion Militis Christiani* (*Handbook of the Christian Soldier*), a work that called for a return to the Bible, not just as the focus of study but as the basis for a disciplined Christian life. This was a call that went against the medieval priority on adherence to the teaching of the institution of the Church and to its elaborate outward trappings of religion. He also penned works promoting the importance of free will, which were his contribution to the well-known vigorous debate with Luther.

The second reason that Erasmus is remembered is related to the first, but is more fundamental. It is his championing of the *ad fontes* method of Renaissance humanism, an approach that characterised the Protestant study of theology and set it in sharp distinction to the scholasticism of the Roman Catholic theologians. The Reformation did not just prosecute certain doctrinal positions over against the Catholic Church, but it also brought an entirely different approach to theological epistemology and the enterprise of Christian scholarship—a fact not often enough recognised. And if it was Luther and Melanchthon who respectively supplied the core doctrines and theological paradigms of the Reformation, it was Erasmus who gave the method.

The *Paraphrases* are perhaps lesser known among Erasmus' works, but they were certainly among the most important for England during the Edwardian and Elizabethan years. They are evidence that he did not just make the call to go back to the Bible, but he also heeded it; the *Paraphrases* are the fruit of Erasmus' own application of the *ad fontes* approach to the study of the New Testament. In them, he attempts to expound the sense and meaning of the biblical books in their own right, taking into account their literary forms and the development of their narratives and arguments. They are not simply the preparation of a manuscript in the original language, nor an argument for a certain theological position, but the close reading and explanation of the original text of the New Testament on its own terms and in context.

The *Paraphrases* in Latin were published between 1517 and 1523, with the translation into English overseen by Nicholas Udall and patronised by Catherine Parr, Henry VIII's last queen.[1] The first completed volume, bringing together the Gospels and Acts, was printed in 1548. The second volume followed in 1549 and contained the remainder of the New Testament, including a paraphrase on Revelation supplied by the Swiss Reformer Leo Jud. Like many of the Reformers, Erasmus seems to have

[1] Among those working with Catherine on the project was a young Princess Mary who translated the Paraphrase of John's Gospel. This throws an interesting light onto Henry's household late in his life.

been wary of Revelation; it was the only book of the New Testament for which he did not provide a *Paraphrase*. In anticipation of the completion of the English translation work, the seventh of Edward VI's 1547 Royal Injunctions says, in part –

> Also that they [members of the clergy] shall provide within three months next after this visitation, one book of the whole Bible, of the largest volume, in English. And within one twelve-months next after the said visitation, the Paraphrasis of Erasmus also in English upon the Gospels, and the same set up in some convenient place, within the said church that they have cure of, whereas their parishioners may most commodiously resort unto the same and read the same.[2]

The same requirement was repeated in the sixth of Elizabeth I's 1559 Injunctions. Thus, at the insistence of the crown, from the mid- to late-sixteenth century, each parish church in England was required to have copies of five books: the Bible, the *Book of Common Prayer*, the two *Books of Homilies* and Erasmus' *Paraphrases* on the Gospels and Acts. In addition to this, the twentieth of Edward's Injunctions required –

> Also that every parson, vicar, curate, chantry priest and stipendiary, being under the degree of Bachelor of Divinity, shall provide and have of his own, within three months after this visitation, the New Testament both in Latin and in English, with Paraphrasis upon the same of Erasmus, and diligently study the same, conferring the one with the other.[3]

This was also repeated in the sixteenth of Elizabeth's Injunctions. Therefore, not only were the common people to have access to the *Paraphrases* on the Gospels and Acts within their churches, the clergy were to own copies of the *Paraphrases* on the entire New Testament.

Intended Purpose

The *Paraphrases* supply a reading, and thus an interpretation, of the entire New Testament, and it was clearly one that was very much in line with the early English Protestants' priorities. Udall makes this quite explicit in his Preface vnto the Kinges Maiestie, there saying –

---

[2] Bray, *Documents*, p 250.

[3] Bray, *Documents*, p 253.

> [Erasmus] bryngeth in and briefly conpriseth the pith of all the mynds & menynges of all the good Doctours of the churche, that ever wrote in justification of feith, in honouryng God onely, in repentaunce and puritie of a Christen mannes lyfe, in detesting of imagerie and corrupte honouryng of Sainctes, in openyng and defacyng the tyrrannie, the blasphemie, Hypocrisie, the ambicion, the usurpacion of the See of Rome, ... in teachyng obedience of the people towardes their rewlers and Governours.[4]

The intention of insisting that the *Paraphrases* on the Gospels and Acts be in every church, and that all lettered clergy should have the *Paraphrases* on the entire New Testament, was the same that lay behind the inclusion of many of the paratexts in the early printed English Bibles: they were to serve as a control on the reading of Scripture. The privilege afforded to them can only be because they were being put forth as the authorised interpretation of the New Testament. If the *First* and *Second Book of Homilies* were designed to repeatedly put forth the approved theological paradigms and ethical convictions of the Church in synthetic form, the *Paraphrases* showed the same through biblical exposition. This understanding is further supported by the fact that the Edwardian Injunction, which required the *Paraphrases* for churches, was simply an expanded version of the parallel Henrician Injunction that had required the Bible (the second Injunction of Henry's second set of Injunctions of 1538). Where Henry had called for Scripture, Edward and Elizabeth called for Scripture plus authorised exposition. There was a difference, however, in how the Bible and the *Paraphrases* would be used; the Bible *had to be* systematically read through in the church services, whereas the *Paraphrases* only needed to be made available for any who were interested in reading them for themselves.

The supply of both Scripture and its sanctioned interpretation is consistent with Cranmer's preface to the *Great Bible* and the preface to the *King's Book*, which had both called for the free reading of the Bible but also for common readers to defer to the Church leaders for its right meaning (see chapter 2). While it may be easy to see this intention in

---

[4] Quoted in J N Wall, 'Godly and Fruitful Lessons: The English Bible, Erasmus' Paraphrases and the Book of Homilies' in J E Booty (ed.), *The Godly Kingdom of Tudor England: Great Books of the English Reformation* (Milton: Morehouse-Barlow, 1981), pp 82–83.

negative light, charity and humility also requires that it is viewed as a protective move, seeking to save the flocks of England from the errors of Rome on the one side and the more radical 'anabaptist' reformers on the other. This would seem to be entirely in keeping with the requirements for church leaders in the New Testament.

Key References

R D Sider et al. (eds), *The Collected Works of Erasmus, Volumes 42–50* (Toronto: University of Toronto Press, 1984–2016)

These volumes are a part of the vast undertaking to prepare modern editions of all of Erasmus' works. The final volume of the *Paraphrases* was produced in 2016, more than 30 years after the first.

The following give good introductions to the *Paraphrases.*

R H Bainton, 'The Paraphrases of Erasmus', *Archiv für Reformationsgeschichte*, 57 (1/2), 1966, pp 67–95

J-F Cottier, 'Erasmus's Paraphrases: A 'New Kind of Commentary'? in Henderson, J.R. (ed.) *The Unfolding Words: Commentary in the Age of Erasmus* (Toronto, Buffalo, London: University of Toronto Press, 2012)

E J Devereux, 'The Publication of the English Paraphrases of Erasmus', *Bulletin of the John Rylands Library*, 51 (2), 1969, pp 348–367

J B Payne et al., 'The Paraphrases of Erasmus: Origin and Character' in R D Sider (ed.), *Collected Works of Erasmus, Volume 42, Paraphrases on Romans and Galatians* (Toronto, Buffalo, London: University of Toronto Press, 1984), pp xi-xix.

A Rabil, *Erasmus and the New Testament: the Mind of a Christian Humanist* (San Antonio: Trinity University Press, 1972)

A Rabil, 'Erasmus's Paraphrases of the New Testament' in R L DeMolen (ed.), *Essays on the Works of Erasmus* (New Haven and London: Yale University Press, 1978)

FOXE'S *ACTS AND MONUMENTS* (*BOOK OF MARTYRS*)

Although popularly known as a 'book of martyrs' because of its extensive records of those who died for the faith—including England's most famous 'Oxford Martyrs'; Cranmer, Latimer and Ridley—the *Acts and Monuments* (*A&M*) is better understood as a history of the church in its struggles from its earliest days through to Foxe's time. It recounts both the history of Christian martyrdom from the time of Stephen and the history of England and its Church from the classical period, with the two streams being merged both historically and theologically.

Running to well over two thousand very large folio pages, the edition produced in 1570 was divided into twelve 'books' and bound in two massive tomes. The first six books take the reader up to the reign of Henry VIII, while the period of 'bloody Mary', for which the work is most famous, is covered in the last three books. Preceding the *A&M* proper is a series of prefaces that include epistles dedicatory and to the readers, a piece explaining Foxe's purpose in writing, a table of the dates of the martyrdoms and a fourfold challenge to papists, against whom the whole work is explicitly pointed. The first half of the first book then lays out a history of the disconnect between Rome and the true Christian church, highlighting some of the major doctrinal errors of the former.

The great catalogue of the faithful martyrs not only dominates the *A&M*, but also distinguishes it. There is no comparable documentary history of the period, and Foxe's approach in compiling the huge number of written records gives the work both its substance and moral gravitas. To a degree, Foxe's work arranges and presents the stories of the martyrs so that they speak for themselves, or at least in support of his agenda.

History

During the reign of Mary I, John Foxe, who was an ordained deacon in the English Church, joined many of the other Protestant leaders who took flight and went into exile on the continent. While in Strasburg in 1554, he printed his *Commentarii Rerum in Ecclesia Gestarum*, a volume he had begun working on in England, which would serve as the seed from which the *A&M* would grow. The *Commentarii* was a two-part history of the reforming movement, with Luther sitting at the hinge point between the first section on the Lollards and the second section on the persecution of the Lutherans. After some time in Frankfurt (where he supported the Knoxians in their dispute with the Coxians), he moved to Basel. There he published his apocalyptic play *Christus Truimphans* and, in 1559, produced the first full version of the *A&M* in Latin. Edmund Grindal, who would later become Elizabeth I's second Archbishop of Canterbury, supplied Foxe with much of its contents. Mozley describes the volume thus –

> Foxe's 1559 book is a folio of 750 pages, divided into six books. The first is a reprint of the Strassburg volume of 1554 with some few additions; the second deals with the reigns of Henry VIII and Edward VI; and the last four treat of the Marian martyrs, whose number Foxe reckons at more than 500. But this third section is no more than a fragment; it ends with the martyrdom of Cranmer of March 21, 1556, and the 150 victims of the last two and half years of the reign form a mere list of names on the concluding four pages of the volume.[5]

Upon returning to England under Elizabeth, Foxe produced the first English edition of the *A&M* in 1563, which differed significantly from the 1559 work. At around 1,800 pages, it had more than doubled in length, largely because it now stretched back to the year 1,000—which Foxe at the time considered to be the end of the pre-apocalyptic biblical millennium—and this enabled Foxe to show the English martyrs as part of a much longer and broader rebellion against Rome. Foxe was keen to engage an audience beyond England and had even planned a companion work to the *A&M,* which would focus on the continental martyrs. While he never completed that task, his friend Henry Pantaleon did in his *Martyrum Historia* of 1563.

Despite the considerable size of this first English volume, it soon became clear to Foxe that it would require further revision as more information was coming into his hands. In 1570, a new edition of the *A&M* appeared. Its relation to the 1563 edition is again well summarised by Mozley –

> All this new information would of course swell his already over-bulky book to a colossal size. Foxe was quite alive to this danger, and again insists on the need of brevity, and to achieve it he cuts out a vast deal of matter—some of it very important—from his 1563 book. He follows Turner's advice

---

[5] J F Mozley, *John Foxe and his Book* (London, Society for Promoting Christian Knowledge, 1940), p 123.

> by getting rid of many Latin documents, but he goes clean against him in refusing to tie himself down to a strict history of the martyrs. In fact he enlarges much more than before upon the general history of church and state, and to crown all he carries his narrative right back to the apostles themselves: for he means to show that protestantism is primitive, and not papalism. He also gives more space to modern continental martyrs, not excluding those of the last seven years; and the number of woodcuts is increased from 60 to 150. The net result is that the new book is not far from double the length of the old.[6]

There were two further editions of the work produced during Foxe's lifetime; one in 1576 and one in 1583, but these only gave rise to minor additions and revisions. Another edition came forward in 1596–7, and there were several more printings in the seventeenth century. In 1571, the Church Canons required that –

> Every archbishop and bishop shall have in his house the Holy Bible in the largest volume, as it was lately printed in London, and also that full and perfect history which is intituled Monuments of martyrs and other such like books fit for the setting forth of religion. These books must be placed either in the hall or in the great chamber, that they may serve to the use of their servants and strangers.[7]

While the canon allows for some flexibility in its call for 'other such like books', this directive indicates the significant esteem in which the *A&M* was held within the English Church. At the behest of the archbishop of Canterbury and the bishops of London and Ely, the mayor and corporation of London ordered the *A&M* to also be set up in orphanages and the halls of city companies. Thus, the *A&M* took its place alongside the lectern Bible and Erasmus' *Paraphrases* as one of the most prominent, and therefore most important, ecclesiastical texts.

---

[6] Mozley, *Foxe*, pp 140–141.

[7] G L Bray (ed.), *The Anglican Canons 1529–1947* (Woodbridge: The Boydell Press, 1998), pp 177–179 cf. p 179, p 183 where essentially the same is required of deans and archdeacons.

Intended Purpose

The *A&M* was more than a collection of stories of the Protestant martyrs; it was also intended as an interpretive narration of the struggles of the true and faithful church, a church that could be correctly identified precisely by its unjust suffering. Foxe's goal was to associate those who died for the faith under Queen Mary with those who had died during the Roman persecutions of the early church. Given that the latter group were universally recognised as being true believers who suffered for the faith, the connection with them would have brought endorsement of the more recent martyrs and sympathy for their theological convictions over and against those of Rome.

Foxe also made a strong theological case for his views based on his understanding of the millennium, with which he opened his work. Following Revelation 20, this period was understood to be a literal thousand years when Satan is restrained and the church is able to exist in relative peace and prosperity, but which ends with his loosing and a new season of corruption in the church and persecution of the faithful. In the first English edition of *A&M,* Foxe followed the then traditional timing, which saw the millennium begin at Christ's resurrection and end with the papacy of Sylvester II. However, by his second edition, he had come to realise that this timing for the millennium would mean that those early believers who died under the persecutions of the Roman Empire were martyred during a time of cosmic peace. To deal with this issue, the 1570 edition of *A&M* recast the millennium as beginning with the establishment of the church by Constantine in 325 and continuing through to the rise of Wycliffe, the 'bright morning star' of the Reformation, in 1325. This meant that the first persecution ended with the Roman Empire's adoption of the true Christian faith and the second began when the Roman Church could no longer tolerate it.[8]

Foxe's revised millennial framework for his martyrology served well to endorse the Protestant movement. But he presented another chronological schema that was not so neat, though no less political: a periodisation of the great ages of history, something not uncommon for

---

[8] Today, both pre- and postmillennialists believe that the thousand years is a still future time, whereas in Foxe's day, it was viewed as a past epoch; most Reformers understood the millennium to cover a significant portion of the history that had already passed between Christ's first advent and their own time.

theologians of his time to discuss. In the first English edition of the *A&M*, this period had four divisions, each progressively worse as the church moved from its 'golden age' under the apostles to its 'brasen age' in his own time. In 1563 this made some sense because, while Mary had died and Elizabeth was reigning, there would not yet have been much confidence in the security of the situation. England had had four monarchs in less than fifteen years, each with their own distinct set of theological convictions, and there was no way of knowing that Elizabeth's reign would end up being as long as stable as it was.

By the second English edition of the *A&M* in 1570, however, there had been over a decade of constancy, so Foxe's cosmic periodisation was changed. In this edition, he outlined five ages of the church since Christ's time, with his present and final stage being a new dawn, rather than the darkest night. Foxe had come to see a new temporal hope for the Church under Elizabeth, something that had been essentially abandoned during the Marian years. However, despite this significant retuning of his eschatological framework, the main point Foxe wanted to communicate remained the same: it was the Reformers who had the true faith, whether that faith was recognised by the way its adherents were persecuted under the Catholics or by the way the nation was safe and secure under more Protestant rule.[9]

Although this goal for the work has a clear political edge, for Foxe, it was also deeply personal. He was not simply calling his readers to accept a Protestant Church and state but to self-examine and be personally convicted of the truth of the Protestant religion. In the preface, 'To the true Christian reader, what vtilitie is to be taken by readyng of these Historyes', he wrote –

[9] Casting his work eschatologically was very likely more than just a practical convenience for Foxe. From a consideration of his whole body of work, it seems that his theology, and entire worldview, were strongly—perhaps dominantly—eschatologically framed. His above-mentioned early play *Christus Triumphans* was, as its name suggests, focused on Christ's final victory over death. In addition, he had worked on a commentary on the book of Revelation which was published posthumously. R Bauckham, *Tudor Apocalypse* (Oxford: The Sutton Courtenay Press, 1978), pp 83–88, says it was likely more important to Foxe than the *A&M* as it gave his primary theological understanding of the meaning of history, whereas the *A&M* really just served as a companion record of history.

> the mild deathes of the Saints do not a little auaile to the stablishing of a good conscience, to learne the contempt of the world, & to come to the feare of God. Moreouer, they confirme faith, encrease godlynes, abate pride in prosperitie, and in aduersitie do open an hope of heauenly comfort. For what man reading the miserie of these godly persons, may not therein as in a glasse behold his owne case, whether he be godly or godles. For if God geue aduersitie vnto a good men, what may either the better sort promise them selues, or the euill not feare? And where as by reading of prophane stories: we are made perhaps more skilfull in warlike affaires: so by reading of this we are made better in our liuings, and besides are better prepared vnto like conflictes, if by Gods permission they shall happen hereafter more wiser by their doctrine, and more stedfast by their example.[10]

Foxe's book was immensely popular in its day. Its formal endorsement by the canons seemed less for the purpose of championing one particular doctrine or another and more about giving credit to the entire Protestant enterprise by supplying a comprehensive narration of its story and forging strong emotional connections with those who had died for the cause. Mozely writes, 'If anything could make England protestant for ever, it would be the memory of the Marian terror; and he desired to burn his dreadful history into the minds of his countrymen both high and low.'[11]

Key References

The entire *A&M* in all of its four editions that were produced during Foxe's lifetime can now be accessed online at *www.johnfoxe.org*

The following give good introductions to the *A&M* and discussions of Foxe's priorities.

E Evenden and T S Freeman, 'Print, Profit and Propaganda: The Elizabethan Privy Council and the 1570 Edition of Foxe's 'Book of

[10] John Foxe, *The Unabridged Acts and Monuments Online* (1576 edition) (HRI Online Publications, Sheffield, 2011). Available from: *http://www.johnfoxe.org,* 1570, preface, p 11.
[11] Mozley, *Foxe,* p 129.

Martyrs'', *The English Historical Review,* 119 (484), 2004, pp 1288–1307

S Felch, 'Shaping the Reader in the Acts and Monuments' in D Loades (ed.), *John Foxe and the English Reformation* (Aldershot: Scolar Press), 1997, pp 52–65

W Haller, *Foxe's Book of Martyrs and the Elect Nation* (London: Jonathan Cape, 1963)

J F Mozley, *John Foxe and his Book* (London: Society for Promoting Christian Knowledge, 1940)

V N Olsen, *John Foxe and the Elizabethan Church* (Berkley, Los Angeles, London: University of California Press, 1973)

H C White, *Tudor Books of Saints and Martyrs* (Madison: The University of Wisconsin Press, 1963)

9. Legal Documents

This brief chapter covers the different types of documents that addressed religious matters and carried some legal authority during England's Reformation. Although lines between Church and state were never very clear cut, three broad seats of authority can be recognised: the Church, with its internal councils and laws, the parliament, representing the people, and the crown, ultimately sitting atop both the spiritual and temporal realms. Because of the mingling of these spheres, theology and doctrine can be found within the various legal documents and records, even if many of them also engage non-religious matters.

Canon Law and Records of Convocations

Canon law is that law which operates within, rather than upon, the Church. It is not the means by which the state regulates the Church, but rather the tool that the Church uses for enforcing its own doctrines. As such, the canon law tends not to supply additional doctrine to that which can be found elsewhere, but it does outline the practical requirements of implementing already existing doctrines, and the penalties for failure to do so. Even so, because the canon laws do engage with doctrines, there are places where they expand upon what is treated more briefly elsewhere. Each collection of canon law is relatively short and easily contained in a single small volume. The laws themselves tend to run from around a paragraph to a couple of pages, with many being half a page or so long.

Convocations were the main meetings of the leadership of the provinces, which were the largest structural units of the national Church. As is the case today, provinces were geographical grouping of dioceses, which in turn were geographical groupings of parishes. Unlike modern Church synods, which tend to have a considerable representation of lay people, convocations were meetings of clergy. In convocation, the clergy were divided into their two houses; the upper house was made up of all of the province's bishops and was overseen by its archbishop, the lower was house was constituted by a representative body of priests, including those serving as deans of cathedrals and archdeacons. The two houses discussed various matters of importance to the Church and communicated with each other through a prolocutor, who was a members of the lower house.

Key References

G L Bray (ed.), *The Anglican Canons 1529–1947* (Woodbridge: The Boydell Press, 1998)

G L Bray (ed.), *Tudor Church Reform* (Woodbridge: The Boydell Press, 2000)

These two volumes offer a magnificent introduction to English canon law. They contain the full text of all the canons from the sixteenth to the twentieth centuries, and where that was prepared in Latin, both the original language and a translation are supplied on facing pages. In addition, there is a running technical commentary on all of the canons, comprehensive indices and very useful appendices. Moreover, both volumes have brilliant substantial historical introductions. In short, these are indispensable works for anyone studying canon law.

G L Bray, 'Canon Law and the Church of England' in A. Milton (ed.) *The Oxford History of Anglicanism, Volume I Reformation and Identity c.1520–1662 (Oxford*: Oxford University Press, 2017), pp 168–185

This is Bray's chapter-length consideration of canon law.

G L Bray (ed.), *Records of Convocation*, 20 vols, (Woodbridge: Boydell and Brewer, 2005–2006)

These volumes span over 500 years of convocations in England, and nearly a millennium in total. The volumes most relevant to the Reformation period are *Volume 7: Canterbury 1509–1603*, and *Volume 14: York 1461–1625*.

Royal Injunctions and Proclamations

The Royal Injunctions prescribed the practical measures that needed to be taken in order to apply the Church's doctrines at the local level. They may be helpfully understood as occupying a place between the published doctrines, such as those found in the *Articles of Religion*, and canon law. Where the *Articles of Religion* laid out what was to be believed, the Injunctions explained how these beliefs would be manifest in the life of the Church, and the canon law then set down the judicial penalties for failure to implement them. This relationship between these formularies cannot always be so neatly mapped, but the general pattern holds.

The Injunctions served to set the theological tone of each monarch's reign. This is clear for Edward VI and Elizabeth I, whose Injunctions were published in the year that each came to the throne (1547 and 1559 respectively). Mary I's Injunctions were published in 1554, the year after her accession. Henry VIII's two sets of Injunctions of 1536 and 1538 can also be understood as coming at the start of his taking full control of the Church for the first time, following the Reformation Parliament.

Proclamations had similar force to the Injunctions, but were produced more occasionally.

Key References

G L Bray (ed.), *Documents of the English Reformation* (Cambridge: James Clarke & Co Ltd, 2004)

This volume prints the full text of all of the Tudor Royal Injunctions.

P L Hughes and J F Larkin (eds), *Tudor Royal Proclamations, Volume 1: The Early Tudors (1485–1553)*, (New Haven and London: Yale University Press: 1964)

P L Hughes and J F Larkin (eds), *Tudor Royal Proclamations, Volume 2: The Later Tudors (1553–1587)*, (New Haven and London: Yale University Press: 1969)

These two volumes print the full text of the Tudor Royal Proclamations in modern English.

Acts of Parliament

Although parliament dealt with a great many matters other than religion, any religious development that was to be made into law needed to be passed by it. Best known to scholars of Tudor Church history are the acts of the Reformation Parliament, including the Act in Restraint of Appeals, the Act of Succession and the Act of Supremacy, and also the Acts of Uniformity that required the *Books of Common Prayer* to be used throughout the realms.

Key References

The Statutes of the Realm (London: Dawsons of Pall Mall, 1810–1828)

All of the acts of parliament from the early thirteenth century (thus including the Magna Carta) to the early eighteenth century can be found in this nine volume set. Volume four is split into two parts, and there are also two volumes of indices. The volumes are quite large and rare but, fortunately, all can now be found online, for example at *https://catalog.hathitrust.org/Record/012297566*

G L Bray (ed.), *Documents of the English Reformation* (Cambridge: James Clarke & Co. Ltd, 1994)

This volume contains the statues relevant to the English Reformation.

Concluding Words

Having completed this overview of the founding formularies of the Protestant Church of England, two summary comments can be made to provoke some ongoing thought, discussion and perhaps even action in today's Anglican Churches.

First, as we continually contend for the place of the historic Christian faith within the Anglican Communion, we should recognise that we will only be helped by knowing our own history well. Rightly or wrongly, the Anglican Church is a broad church, its worldwide membership including hard-line evangelicals, advocates of high church traditionalism, charismatics, revisionist liberals and more besides. For some, this breadth is considered a great strength and beauty. For others, it represents an offensive and intolerable compromise. Consequently, Church leaders, scholars, lay people, and even members of the public without any real connection to the Church, invest huge amounts of energy into the debate around the Church's proper identity, and into activities directed towards their version of institutional purification.

In recent times, the need to think deliberately about the nature of 'true Anglicanism' has only become more pressing as some of the expressions of diversity within the Anglican denomination have pulled at the threads that bind its parts, sometimes beyond what it can bear. Different views, not only on the appropriate forms of corporate worship but also on the most fundamental Christian doctrines, have all but formally rent parts of the fabric of the global Anglican Communion.

As the tearing and various attempts at patching continue, arguments for different positions will naturally draw on the Church's history. Too often, however, those calling on the founding documents do not have a great familiarity with them, neither with their interrelatedness nor with their place in the history of the Church of England. As a result, those formularies are not always introduced into the discussions in better-informed or even-handed ways. Conversations will be improved if they include some informed and balanced engagement with the Church's history. If our past did establish truly healthy foundations and set positive long-term trajectories for a constantly reforming Church, it is worth the effort to understand it right so that it can make its full and proper contribution today.

Second, and perhaps more important, is the challenge for today's churches to consider whether or not they are doing all that England knew it needed to do as it worked for the thoroughgoing reform, revitalisation and reception of the faith. While many Anglican leaders continue to use the *Book of Common Prayer* for their regular Sunday services, they may no longer also engage in a full-orbed program of spiritual care. We ought to be involved in systematic catechesis of young people and of those exploring the faith. We ought to be publicly resisting heterodox teaching. We ought to be shaping the worldview of congregants by preaching faithful doctrine. We ought to be ensuring that the Bible is read through and interpreted well in church services. We ought to be encouraging the use of theologically orthodox materials for regular private devotions. We ought to be recounting the stories of the heroes of the Church for the edification of those striving to persevere today. The breadth of formularies produced during the English Reformation is a testament to the Church's commitment to nurture the flock of Christ entrusted to its care in all these ways, and today's Church ought to be doing the same. Even if it is decided that those sixteenth-century documents are now too dated for ongoing use, there should be careful consideration of what might be used in their place.

But it may well be that many of the founding formularies are, in fact, still helpful for the Church today. They were crafted by England's great theologian-churchmen, who were both theologically capable and also conscious of the on-the-ground needs of the local parishes—and who, in many cases, had a blessed capacity to present profound truths with a beautiful, reflective simplicity. From them we have a heritage surely worth embracing—at least at the level of intent, if not also in form. The formularies are their legacy to us. We do well to receive them eagerly.

If you have enjoyed this book, you might like to consider:

- supporting the work of the Latimer Trust
- reading more of our publications
- recommending them to others

See www.latimertrust.org for more information.

Latimer Studies

LS 01	The Evangelical Anglican Identity Problem	Jim Packer
LS 02	The ASB Rite A Communion: A Way Forward	Roger Beckwith
LS 03	The Doctrine of Justification in the Church of England	Robin Leaver
LS 04	Justification Today: The Roman Catholic and Anglican Debate	R. G. England
LS 05/06	Homosexuals in the Christian Fellowship	David Atkinson
LS 07	Nationhood: A Christian Perspective	O. R. Johnston
LS 08	Evangelical Anglican Identity: Problems and Prospects	Tom Wright
LS 09	Confessing the Faith in the Church of England Today	Roger Beckwith
LS 10	A Kind of Noah's Ark? The Anglican Commitment to Comprehensiveness	Jim Packer
LS 11	Sickness and Healing in the Church	Donald Allister
LS 12	Rome and Reformation Today: How Luther Speaks to the New Situation	James Atkinson
LS 13	Music as Preaching: Bach, Passions and Music in Worship	Robin Leaver
LS 14	Jesus Through Other Eyes: Christology in a Multi-faith Context	Christopher Lamb
LS 15	Church and State Under God	James Atkinson,
LS 16	Language and Liturgy	Gerald Bray, Steve Wilcockson, Robin Leaver
LS 17	Christianity and Judaism: New Understanding, New Relationship	James Atkinson
LS 18	Sacraments and Ministry in Ecumenical Perspective	Gerald Bray
LS 19	The Functions of a National Church	Max Warren
LS19 (2nd ed.)	British Values and the National Church: Essays on Church and State from 1964-2014	Ed. David Holloway
LS 20/21	The Thirty-Nine Articles: Their Place and Use Today	Jim Packer, Roger Beckwith

LS 22	How We Got Our Prayer Book	T.W. Drury, Roger Beckwith
LS 23/24	Creation or Evolution: a False Antithesis?	Mike Poole, Gordon Wenham
LS 25	Christianity and the Craft	Gerard Moate
LS 26	ARCIC II and Justification	Alister McGrath
LS 27	The Challenge of the Housechurches	Tony Higton, Gilbert Kirby
LS 28	Communion for Children? The Current Debate	A. A. Langdon
LS 29/30	Theological Politics	Nigel Biggar
LS 31	Eucharistic Consecration in the First Four Centuries and its Implications for Liturgical Reform	Nigel Scotland
LS 32	A Christian Theological Language	Gerald Bray
LS 33	Mission in Unity: The Bible and Missionary Structures	Duncan McMann
LS 34	Stewards of Creation: Environmentalism in the Light of Biblical Teaching	Lawrence Osborn
LS 35/36	Mission and Evangelism in Recent Thinking: 1974-1986	Robert Bashford
LS 37	Future Patterns of Episcopacy: Reflections in Retirement	Stuart Blanch
LS 38	Christian Character: Jeremy Taylor and Christian Ethics Today	David Scott
LS 39	Islam: Towards a Christian Assessment	Hugh Goddard
LS 40	Liberal Catholicism: Charles Gore and the Question of Authority	G. F. Grimes
LS 41/42	The Christian Message in a Multi-faith Society	Colin Chapman
LS 43	The Way of Holiness 1: Principles	D. A. Ousley
LS 44/45	The Lambeth Articles	V. C. Miller
LS 46	The Way of Holiness 2: Issues	D. A. Ousley
LS 47	Building Multi-Racial Churches	John Root
LS 48	Episcopal Oversight: A Case for Reform	David Holloway
LS 49	Euthanasia: A Christian Evaluation	Henk Jochemsen
LS 50/51	The Rough Places Plain: AEA 1995	
LS 52	A Critique of Spirituality	John Pearce
LS 53/54	The Toronto Blessing	Martyn Percy

LS 55	The Theology of Rowan Williams	Garry Williams
LS 56/57	Reforming Forwards? The Process of Reception and the Consecration of Woman as Bishops	Peter Toon
LS 58	The Oath of Canonical Obedience	Gerald Bray
LS 59	The Parish System: The Same Yesterday, Today And For Ever?	Mark Burkill
LS 60	'I Absolve You': Private Confession and the Church of England	Andrew Atherstone
LS 61	The Water and the Wine: A Contribution to the Debate on Children and Holy Communion	Roger Beckwith, Andrew Daunton-Fear
LS 62	Must God Punish Sin?	Ben Cooper
LS 63	Too Big For Words? The Transcendence of God and Finite Human Speech	Mark D. Thompson
LS 64	A Step Too Far: An Evangelical Critique of Christian Mysticism	Marian Raikes
LS 65	The New Testament and Slavery: Approaches and Implications	Mark Meynell
LS 66	The Tragedy of 1662: The Ejection and Persecution of the Puritans	Lee Gatiss
LS 67	Heresy, Schism & Apostasy	Gerald Bray
LS 68	Paul in 3D: Preaching Paul as Pastor, Story-teller and Sage	Ben Cooper
LS69	Christianity and the Tolerance of Liberalism: J.Gresham Machen and the Presbyterian Controversy of 1922-1937	Lee Gatiss
LS70	An Anglican Evangelical Identity Crisis: The Churchman–Anvil Affair of 1981-4	Andrew Atherstone
LS71	Empty and Evil: The worship of other faiths in 1 Corinthians 8-10 and today	Rohintan Mody
LS72	To Plough or to Preach: Mission Strategies in New Zealand during the 1820s	Malcolm Falloon
LS73	Plastic People: How Queer Theory is changing us	Peter Sanlon
LS74	Deification and Union with Christ: Salvation in Orthodox and Reformed thought	Slavko Eždenci
LS75	As It Is Written: Interpreting the Bible with Boldness	Benjamin Sargent
LS76	Light From Dark Ages? An Evangelical Critique of Celtic Spirituality	Marian Raikes
LS77	The Ethics of Usury	Ben Cooper

LS78	For Us and For Our Salvation: 'Limited Atonement' in the Bible, Doctrine, History and Ministry	Lee Gatiss
LS79	Positive Complementarianism: The Key Biblical Texts	Ben Cooper
LS80	Were they Preaching 'Another Gospel'? Justification by faith in the Second Century	Andrew Daunton-Fear
LS81	Thinking Aloud: Responding to the Contemporary Debate about Marriage, Sexuality and Reconciliation	Martin Davie
LS82	Spells, Sorcerers and Spirits: Magic and the Occult in the Bible	Kirsten Birkett
LS83	Your Will Be Done: Exploring Eternal Subordination, Divine Monarchy and Divine Humility	M.J Ovey
LS84	Resilience: A Spiritual Project	Kirsten Birkett
LS85	Anglican Elders? Locally shared pastoral leadership in English Anglican Churches	Ed Moll

Latimer Briefings

LB01	The Church of England: What it is, and what it stands for	R. T. Beckwith
LB02	Praying with Understanding: Explanations of Words and Passages in the Book of Common Prayer	R. T. Beckwith
LB03	The Failure of the Church of England? The Church, the Nation and the Anglican Communion	A. Pollard
LB04	Towards a Heritage Renewed	H.R.M. Craig
LB05	Christ's Gospel to the Nations: The Heart & Mind of Evangelicalism Past, Present & Future	Peter Jensen
LB06	Passion for the Gospel: Hugh Latimer (1485–1555) Then and Now. A commemorative lecture to mark the 450th anniversary of his martyrdom in Oxford	A. McGrath
LB07	Truth and Unity in Christian Fellowship	Michael Nazir-Ali
LB08	Unworthy Ministers: Donatism and Discipline Today	Mark Burkill
LB09	Witnessing to Western Muslims: A Worldview Approach to Sharing Faith	Richard Shumack

LB10	Scarf or Stole at Ordination? A Plea for the Evangelical Conscience	Andrew Atherstone
LB11	How to Write a Theology Essay	Michael P. Jensen
LB12	Preaching: A Guidebook for Beginners	Allan Chapple
LB13	Justification by Faith: Orientating the Church's teaching and practice to Christ (Toon Lecture 1)	Michael Nazir-Ali
LB14	"Remember Your Leaders": Principles and Priorities for Leaders from Hebrews 13	Wallace Benn
LB15	How the Anglican Communion came to be and where it is going	Michael Nazir-Ali
LB16	Divine Allurement: Cranmer's Comfortable Words	Ashley Null
LB17	True Devotion: In Search of Authentic Spirituality	Allan Chapple
LB18	Commemorating War and Praying for Peace: A Christian reflection on the Armed Forces	John Neal
LB19	A Better Vision: Resources for the debate about human sexuality in the Church of England	Ed. Martin Davie
LB20	Transgender Liturgies: Should the Church of England develop liturgical materials to mark gender transition?	Martin Davie
LB22	Ministry Under the Microscope: The What, Why, and How of Christian Ministry	Allan Chapple

Anglican Foundations Series

FWC	The Faith We Confess: An Exposition of the 39 Articles	Gerald Bray
AF02	The 'Very Pure Word of God': The Book of Common Prayer as a Model of Biblical Liturgy	Peter Adam
AF03	Dearly Beloved: Building God's People Through Morning and Evening Prayer	Mark Burkill
AF04	Day by Day: The Rhythm of the Bible in the Book of Common Prayer	Benjamin Sargent
AF05	The Supper: Cranmer and Communion	Nigel Scotland
AF06	A Fruitful Exhortation: A Guide to the Homilies	Gerald Bray
AF07	Instruction in the Way of the Lord: A Guide to the Prayer Book Catechism	Martin Davie
AF08	Till Death Us Do Part: "The Solemnization of Matrimony" in the Book of Common Prayer	Simon Vibert
AF09	'Sure and Certain Hope': Death and Burial in the Book of Common Prayer	Andrew Cinnamond

Latimer Books

GGC	God, Gays and the Church: Human Sexuality and Experience in Christian Thinking	eds. Lisa Nolland, Chris Sugden, Sarah Finch
WTL	The Way, the Truth and the Life: Theological Resources for a Pilgrimage to a Global Anglican Future	eds. Vinay Samuel, Chris Sugden, Sarah Finch
AEID	Anglican Evangelical Identity – Yesterday and Today	J.I.Packer, N.T.Wright
IB	The Anglican Evangelical Doctrine of Infant Baptism	John Stott, Alec Motyer
BF	Being Faithful: The Shape of Historic Anglicanism Today	Theological Resource Group of GAFCON
TPG	The True Profession of the Gospel: Augustus Toplady and Reclaiming our Reformed Foundations	Lee Gatiss
SG	Shadow Gospel: Rowan Williams and the Anglican Communion Crisis	Charles Raven
TTB	Translating the Bible: From William Tyndale to King James	Gerald Bray
PWS	Pilgrims, Warriors, and Servants: Puritan Wisdom for Today's Church	ed. Lee Gatiss
PPA	Preachers, Pastors, and Ambassadors: Puritan Wisdom for Today's Church	ed. Lee Gatiss
CWP	The Church, Women Bishops and Provision: The Integrity of Orthodox Objections to the Proposed Legislation Allowing Women Bishops	
TSF	The Truth Shall Set You Free: Global Anglicans in the 21st Century	ed. Charles Raven
LMM	Launching Marsden's Mission: The Beginnings of the Church Missionary Society in New Zealand, viewed from New South Wales	eds. Peter G Bolt David B. Pettett
MST1	Listen To Him: Reading and Preaching Emmanuel in Matthew	Ed. Peter Bolt

GWC	The Genius of George Whitefield: Reflections on his Ministry from 21st Century Africa	Ed. Benjamin Dean & Adriaan Neele
LDBN	The Legacy of David Broughton Knox	Ed. Edward Loane

Printed in the USA
CPSIA information can be obtained
at www.ICGtesting.com
LVHW091044280124
769969LV00002B/467

9 781906 327538